Leading Edge Essays On AI And Law

Advanced Series On
Artificial Intelligence (AI)
And Law

Dr. Lance B. Eliot, MBA, PhD

Disclaimer: This book is presented solely for educational and entertainment purposes. The author and publisher are not offering it as legal, accounting, or other professional services advice. The author and publisher make no representations or warranties of any kind and assume no liabilities of any kind with respect to the accuracy or completeness of the contents and specifically disclaim any implied warranties of merchantability or fitness of use for a particular purpose. Neither the author nor the publisher shall be held liable or responsible to any person or entity with respect to any loss or incidental or consequential damages caused, or alleged to have been caused, directly or indirectly, by the information or programs contained herein. Every company is different and the advice and strategies contained herein may not be suitable for your situation.

ISBN: 978-1-95-738604-1

DEDICATION

To my incredible daughter, Lauren, and my incredible son, Michael.

Forest fortuna adiuvat (from the Latin; good fortune favors the brave).

CONTENTS

Note: Visuals are collected together in Appendix B, rather than being interjected into the chapter contents, for ease of reading, enhanced flow, and to see the visuals altogether.

ACKNOWLEDGMENTS

I have been the beneficiary of advice and counsel by many friends, colleagues, family, investors, and many others. I want to thank everyone that has aided me throughout my career. I write from the heart and the head, having experienced first-hand what it means to have others around you that support you during the good times and the tough times.

To renowned scholar and colleague, Dr. Warren Bennis, I offer my deepest thanks and appreciation, especially for his calm and insightful wisdom and support.

To billionaire and university trustee, Mark Stevens and his generous efforts toward funding and supporting the Stevens Center for Innovation.

To Peter Drucker, William Wang, Aaron Levie, Peter Kim, Jon Kraft, Cindy Crawford, Jenny Ming, Steve Milligan, Chis Underwood, Frank Gehry, Buzz Aldrin, Steve Forbes, Bill Thompson, Dave Dillon, Alan Fuerstman, Larry Ellison, Jim Sinegal, John Sperling, Mark Stevenson, Anand Nallathambi, Thomas Barrack, Jr., and many other innovators and leaders that I have met and gained mightily from doing so.

Thanks to Ed Trainor, Kevin Anderson, James Hickey, Wendell Jones, Ken Harris, DuWayne Peterson, Mike Brown, Jim Thornton, Abhi Beniwal, Al Biland, John Nomura, Eliot Weinman, John Desmond, and many others for their unwavering support during my career.

Thanks goes to the Stanford University CodeX Center for Legal Informatics and the Stanford University Computer Science department for their generous support, and for the insightfual and inspirational discussions and feedback from my many fellow colleagues there.

And most of all thanks as always to Lauren and Michael, for their ongoing support and for having seen me writing and heard much of this material during the many months involved in writing it. To their patience and willingness to listen.

CHAPTER 1
INTRODUCTION TO AI AND LAW

This book provides a series of crucial essays encompassing the burgeoning field of AI and the law.

These essays are ostensibly standalone and do not require any prior familiarity with the AI and law topic. You are welcome to read the essays in whichever order you might prefer. The essays have been numbered and sequenced as chapters for ease of referring to the discussions and not due to any need to read one before another.

The essays provide a helpful overview and entry point into the field of AI and law. You will find the essays relatively easy to read and eschew arcane techno-terminology, aiming to layout the vital aspects in clear language and seeking to be readily grasped. The chosen topics entail the latest and hottest trends in the AI and law arena.

For those of you that are potentially interested in knowing more about AI and the law in a deeper way, you might consider my two other books on this subject:

- *"AI and Legal Reasoning Essentials"* by Dr. Lance Eliot
- *"Artificial Intelligence and LegalTech Essentials"* by Dr. Lance Eliot

Those are more akin to textbook-style orientations to the AI and the law field. Both books are available on Amazon and at major bookseller sites. The first book listed provides a comprehensive and detailed exploration of AI and law, while the second book tends to focus primarily on LegalTech and the blending of AI.

One of the most frequent questions that I get asked during my webinars, seminars, and college courses about AI and the law consists of what the phrase "AI and the law" actually refers to.

That's a fair question and deserves a useful answer. In a moment, I will borrow from my other books to provide an explanation about the meaning of "AI and the law" and then dovetail into a brief indication about each of the essays contained in this collection.

Per the essays, you'll end up seeing that there is a great deal of enthusiastic spirit for AI and the law, and likewise a sizable dollop of angst and trepidation about the intertwining of the two. In my view, whether you love it or hate it, there is no stopping the steamroller moving ahead that is going to infuse AI together with the law.

I would urge that any lawyer worth their salt ought to be learning about AI and the law. This will assuredly be especially important for those that are just now starting their legal careers, which I mention because the odds are that the convergence of AI and the law will have an especially pronounced effect throughout your lifelong legal efforts.

For those of you that might be going a more so academic route in the legal realm, rather than being a practitioner of the law per se, the beauty of AI and the law is that there is ample room for new research and a grand opportunity to make a demonstrative mark on the field.

Despite the fact that the field of AI and the law has been studied for many years, dating back to the beginning of the AI field itself, please be aware that we have only scratched the surface on this interweaving. Anyone with a desire to push the boundaries of these two realms will readily find plenty of rampways to do so.

If you are curious about the possible research avenues to pursue, make sure to take a look at my book on *AI and Legal Reasoning Essentials* since it provides a solid foundation on the research to-date and postulates what might be coming down the pike in future research activities. I bid you welcome to the field and wish you the best of luck in your endeavors.

AI And Law

In my viewpoint, Artificial Intelligence (AI) and the field of law are synergistic partners. The intertwining of AI and Law can generally be categorized into two major approaches:

- **AI as applied to Law**
- **Law as applied to AI**

Let us consider each of those two approaches.

AI As Applied To Law

AI as applied to law consists of trying to utilize AI technologies and AI techniques for the embodiment of law, potentially being able to perform legal tasks and undertake legal reasoning associated with the practice of law. Those scholars, experts, and practitioners that have this focus are using AI to aid or integrate artificial intelligence into how humans practice law, either augmenting lawyers and other legal professionals or possibly replacing them in the performance of various legal tasks.

Crafting such AI is especially hard to accomplish, problematic in many ways, and there have been and continue to emerge a myriad of attempts to achieve this difficult goal or aspiration. The rise of LegalTech and LawTech, which is modern digital technology used to support and enable lawyers, law offices, and the like throughout the practice of law are gradually and inexorably being bolstered by the addition of AI capabilities.

There are many indications already of this trend rapidly expanding in the existing and growing LegalTech and LawTech marketplace. Notably, the potent AI and LegalTech/LawTech combination has been drawing the rapt attention of Venture Capitalists (VCs). According to figures by the National Venture Capital Association (NVCA), the last several years have witnessed VC's making key investments of over one billion dollars towards law-related tech startups, many of which have some form of an AI capability involved.

Most of the AI developed so far for LegalTech and LawTech is only able to assist lawyers and legal professions in rather modest and simplistic ways. For example, AI might speed-up the search for documents during e-discovery or might enhance the preparation of a contract by identifying pertinent contractual language from a corpus of prior contracts.

Where the field of applying AI to law is seeking to head involves having AI that can perform legal minded tasks that human lawyers and other legal professionals perform. In essence, creating AI systems that can undertake legal reasoning. This is commonly referred to as AI for Legal Reasoning (AILR).

In a sense, legal reasoning goes to the core of performing legal tasks and is considered the ultimate pinnacle as it were for the efforts to try and apply AI to law. It is undoubtedly one of the most exciting areas of the AI-applied-to-law arena and one that holds both tremendous promise and perhaps some angst and possible somber qualms.

Law As Applied To AI

The other major approach that combines AI and law focuses on the law as applied AI. This is an equally crucial perspective on the AI and law topic.

Sometimes this is also referred to as the **Governance of AI**, though there are those that believe that to be a somewhat narrower perspective on the topic. In any case, the focus is primarily on the governance of AI and how our laws might need to be revised, updated, or revamped in light of AI systems.

You likely already know that AI is experiencing quite a resurgence and has become a key focus of the tech field, along with gaining attention throughout society. AI is being rapidly infused into a wide variety of industries and domain specialties, including AI in the financial sector, AI in the medical domain, and so on.

This rapid pace of AI adoption has opened the eyes of society about the benefits of AI but also has gradually brought to the forefront many of the costs or negative aspects that AI can bring forth. Some assert that our existing laws are insufficient to cope with the advances that AI is producing.

Thus, the need to closely examine our existing laws and possibly revamp them for an era and future of ubiquitous AI.

Expected Impacts

Let's consider how AI and the law can impact those in the AI field, and also contemplate how it can impact those in the field of law.

If you are an AI specialist, you should certainly be interested in the AI and law topic, either due to the possibilities of advancing AI by discovering how to leverage AI into the legal domain or due to the potential of how existing and future laws are going to impact the exploration and fielding of AI systems.

If you are a lawyer or legal specialist, you ought to be interested in the AI and law topic too, for the same reasons as the AI specialist, though perhaps with some added stake in the game.

What is the added stake?

If AI can ultimately become advanced enough to practice law, there is concern by some that it could potentially replace the need for human lawyers and other human legal-related law practitioners.

Some liken this to the famous and telling remark about commitment as exhibited via a chicken and a pig. A chicken and a pig are walking along and discussing what they might do together, and the chicken offers that perhaps they ought to open a restaurant that serves ham-n-eggs. Upon a moment of reflection, the pig speaks up and says that if they did so, the chicken would only be involved (making the eggs), while the pig would end-up being fully committed (being the bacon).

In that sense, AI specialists in this topic are involved, while legal specialists and lawyers are committed.

Meanwhile, for those of you squarely in the field of law, lest you think that AI specialists are to be spared the same fate of being overtaken by AI, you will be perhaps surprised to know that there are efforts underway to craft AI that makes AI, such as in the field of Machine Learning (ML), a specialty known as AutoML, which could potentially put human developers of AI out of a job.

What is good for the goose is good for the gander. Or, it might be that what is bad for the goose is equally bad for the gander.

About These Essays

Now that you've gotten an initial synopsis regarding the topic of AI and law, let's take a moment to briefly take a look at the essays assembled for this decisive collection.

Chapter 1 – Introduction To AI And Law

Key briefing points about this chapter:

- This book is a collection of crucial essays about AI and the law
- The essays are provided as numbered chapters (the sequence is not essential)
- AI and the law consist of two key facets
- One facet is AI as applied to the law (a mainstay of this collection)
- The other facet is applying the law to AI (i.e., governance of AI)

Chapter 2 - AI & Law: Legal Storytelling

Key briefing points about this chapter:

- Some attorneys are trained to do just-the-facts legal arguments
- Only recently has such training also encompassed the skills of legal storytelling
- Composing and conveying a sufficient legal story can make or break a legal case
- Lawyers often do not have the inclination nor time to put together such stories
- Into this void comes the use of AI-based legal storytelling apps

Chapter 3 - AI & Law: Lawyer Generalists

Key briefing points about this chapter:

- A thorny question for attorneys consists of whether to specialize or not
- There are a variety of legal specializations to choose from
- Some say it is better to remain as a generalized legal practitioner of the law
- There are numerous tradeoffs to consider
- One surprising factor involves the emergence of AI in the law

Chapter 4 – AI & Law: NP Equals P Question

Key briefing points about this chapter:

- There is an important open question in the computer science field worth pondering
- Simply stated, the question is whether NP equals P (does NP = P?)
- Turns out that is a quite difficult problem to answer
- If we knew the answer it would make a big difference for AI
- And would make a big difference for the use of AI in the law

Chapter 5 - AI & Law: If-Then Cornerstone

Key briefing points about this chapter:

- The use of If-Then statements is a cornerstone underlying the history of law
- Most famous perhaps is the code of laws established by Hammurabi
- During the initial days of applying AI to the law, the If-Then was king
- The If-Then fell out of favor and gave way to machine learning techniques
- If-Then revival is underway and typified by the common-sense atlas of ATOMIC

Chapter 6 - AI & Law: Legal Bans On AI

Key briefing points about this chapter:

- Recent clamor indicates increasing pressures to ban AI in various respects
- All out bans on AI are rarer and generally untenable
- The United Nations has gotten onto the ban AI bandwagon
- You can expect a need for lawyers versed in legal elements of AI to be highly sought
- Some will aid in crafting new regulations, others will aid firms deploying AI, etc.

Chapter 7 - AI & Law: AI Bill Of Rights

Key briefing points about this chapter:

- A cornerstone of our existent laws and society is embodied in the U.S. Bill of Rights
- Lawyers especially are versed in the nuances of the Bill of Rights
- Today's spreading of AI is worrisome that our basic rights are being violated
- Some suggest that we need an augmented AI-oriented bill of rights
- Such an effort is underway by the White House Office of Science and Technology Policy (OSTP)

Chapter 8 - AI & Law: Autonomous AI Bans

Key briefing points about this chapter:

- AI has gotten into trouble and transcended the initial professed welcoming
- We have discovered that AI systems can embed all kinds of unsavory aspects
- Debates about what type of AI should be legally banned is an ongoing exercise
- It might seem obvious that a legal ban on AI for autonomous weapons should occur
- A close look at the autonomous weapons issue showcases tradeoffs exist even there

Chapter 9 – AI & Law: AI Robo-Artist Copyrights

Key briefing points about this chapter:

- There are plenty of copyright laws globally that serve to provide authorship protections
- Copyright goes to the creator of a novel work of art, music, literary narrative, etc.
- We naturally assume that a copyright can be held only by humans and not by non-humans
- Some ardently believe that AI ought to be permitted as a valid copyright holder
- Ongoing and strident legal debates on this are underway and not easily resolved

Chapter 10 - AI & Law: Attorney Workloads

Key briefing points about this chapter:

- Attorney workloads are notoriously high and at times bone crushing of mind and body
- On the surface, this seems fine as long as the hours are billable and making money
- Issues undercutting this include attorney burnout, heightened turnover, etc.
- AI and especially Machine Learning can be used to analyze attorney workloads
- Insights gleaned allow for workload balancing, plus spark use of AI-infused LegalTech

Chapter 11 - AI & Law: Do Laws Cover AI

Key briefing points about this chapter:

- There was a time that *AI For Good* was captivating worldwide attention
- A bubble was burst upon the realization that *AI For Bad* also is taking place
- Into this morass comes the question of whether existing laws handle AI sufficiently
- One camp says our laws don't, while the other extreme camp says our laws do
- Using an existence proof ostensibly highlights a vital in-between nature thereof

Chapter 12 - AI & Law: Turbo-Encabulator

Key briefing points about this chapter:

- The turbo-encabulator dates back to the 1940s (be wary)
- Every few years since then, the turbo-encabulator seems to resurface
- We can use the turbo-encabulator to consider the status of AI in the law
- This is especially relevant given the advent of AI and Machine Learning in the law
- Important lessons are worthy of consideration and reflection thereof

Chapter 13 – AI & Law: Assembly Line Lawyering

Key briefing points about this chapter:

- Assembly lines are well-known as being key to efficient mass production
- Manufacturing extensively uses assembly lines, as do fast-food eateries
- Concerns have been raised about assembly line pitfalls in our justice system
- Some have floated the notion of assembly lines in law practices for legal endeavors
- AI in the law could very likely spur and enable such law practice transformations

Chapter 14 – AI & Law: AI Forensics Vulnerabilities

Key briefing points about this chapter:

- Most lawyers will inevitably encounter digital photos or digital video in their legal cases
- Forensic specialists are often hired to inspect the digital imagery
- These inspections can also entail digital transformations, such as enlarging images
- AI and especially Machine Learning are often the workhorse doing the transforms
- Lawyers need to realize that there are legally open questions that can arise

Chapter 15 - AI & Law: Explainable AI Meaningfulness

Key briefing points about this chapter:

- AI continues to be rolled out in an ever-increasing number of avenues
- Often, the AI contains algorithmic decision making (ADM) rendering key decisions
- Regulators are rapidly seeking to ensure that the AI also provides ADM explanations
- This is known as XAI or explainable AI
- For XAI, the notion of legal meaningfulness is becoming a core characteristic

Chapter 16 – AI & Law: Legal Sugar

Key briefing points about this chapter:

- Software engineers are familiar with the likes of so-called syntactic sugar
- This consists of embellishing program code for hopefully added clarity
- The semantics remain unchanged, just the syntax has been altered in cosmetic ways
- Perhaps our laws could benefit from having some syntactic sugaring take place
- AI for this purpose can be devised, though will struggle with averting semantic pitfalls

Chapter 17 - AI & Law: Legal Latin Keystones

Key briefing points about this chapter:

- Lawyers are usually well versed in the cornerstone precepts of today's rule of law
- These are now famous legal precepts that stem from earlier Latin terminology
- For example, we accept at face value that there shall be no penalty without law
- In the push toward using AI to embody the law, we need to keep such precepts in mind
- AI must be devised such that ensures these bedrock principles remain intact and active

Chapter 18 - AI & Law: AI Jury Simulations

Key briefing points about this chapter:

- Juries and juror behavior is vital factor for lawyers and lawyering
- Jury research has been ongoing since the earliest days of jury trials
- A prevailing approach has been the use of mock jurors in simulated trials
- Advances in computing have led to remote online mock jury research efforts
- AI is taking the mock jury to a new level and will transform jury research

Chapter 19 - AI & Law: AI As Thirteenth Juror

Key briefing points about this chapter:

- There is no doubt that a jury trial is one of the cornerstones of our form of adjudication
- Twelve jurors are the usual standard, all of whom are expected to act impartially
- A popular catchphrase involves referring to a thirteenth juror
- Besides a metaphorical reference, some argue that we do in fact need to add a juror
- Though the assumption is that the 13th juror is a human, perhaps AI will suffice instead

Chapter 20 - AI & Law: Jury Contamination And Misconduct

Key briefing points about this chapter:

- We can likely all agree that a core precept of our laws is the right to a trial by jury
- Not just any jury will do per se, since we also require a fair and impartial jury
- Pretrial contamination can adversely affect the fair and impartial aspiration
- During the trial, there can be further contamination, along with juror misconduct
- Various methods are used to detect these juror transgressions, including now AI

Chapter 21 - AI & Law: Juror Impartiality

Key briefing points about this chapter:

- Trial by jury is a cornerstone of our judicial beliefs and adjudication ecosystem
- Jurors are required to be and remain impartial throughout a trial
- Sometimes a juror takes overt acts that reveal they are not impartial
- Other times a juror might subtly shift beyond impartiality
- A vexing question is whether the use of AI in the courtroom could spur juror partiality

Chapter 22 – AI & Law: Chewbacca Defense

Key briefing points about this chapter:

- Lawyers have likely seen their fill of inane arguments that veer into being nonsensical
- A handy and popular catchphrase for such argumentation is the Chewbacca defense
- The naming is from a famous South Park episode that skewered the O.J. Simpson case
- Shifting gears, AI-based legal reasoning systems can aid the crafting of legal arguments
- A vexing question is whether the AI should offer any Chewbacca defense suggestions

Chapter 23 - AI & Law: Legal Ops CLOC 12

Key briefing points about this chapter:

- Attorneys typically focus initially after law school on practicing law per se
- The surrounding aspects of running a law practice is not especially top of mind
- An inadequately run law practice is likely to collapse and undercut the lawyering
- Legal operations also known as Legal Ops is key, as typified by the CLOC 12 functions
- Turns out that AI applies to lawyering and all of the Legal Ops activities

Chapter 24 - AI & Law: Deep Legal Knowledge

Key briefing points about this chapter:

- Earlier uses of AI focused on the use of rule-based expert systems and knowledge bases
- Current approaches tend to exploit Machine Learning and artificial neural networks
- A problem with Machine Learning is that it tends to be a mathematical enigma of sorts
- For topmost chess playing games, recent efforts have probed the artificial neural networks
- The same probing needs to be done with AI-based legal reasoning systems

Chapter 25 - AI & Law: Superhuman AI

Key briefing points about this article:

- The catchphrase of being superhuman has crept into our everyday lexicon
- Part of this emergence is due to the advent of modern-day AI systems
- When an AI system seems to have exceeded human capacities, it gets the superhuman title
- Turns out that there is no accepted common definition for the superhuman AI notion
- We are woefully witnessing increasing claims of so-called superhuman AI-based lawyering

More About This Book

For anyone opting to use this book in a class or course that pertains to these topics, note that Appendix A contains suggestions about how to use the book in a classroom setting.

Furthermore, Appendix B contains a set of slides that depict many of the salient points made throughout the book.

In some of my prior books, I've interspersed the slides into the chapter contents, but feedback by readers has generally been that readers prefer to not have the textual flow become disrupted by the slides, and instead prefer to have the supplemental material assembled altogether into an appendix.

To make sure that you are aware of those added materials, you'll notice that the ending of each chapter provides a quick reminder about the visual depictions that are available in Appendix B.

And so, with this overall orientation to the nature and structure of this book in mind, please proceed to read the essays and learn about the field of AI and law. I'm truly hoping that you'll find the essays mentally engaging and stimulative to the nature of how the law is being practiced and what the future of the law might become.

Note: *For supplemental materials depicting the aspects discussed in this chapter, refer to Appendix B, which contains various augmented diagrams, charts, and additional related facets of relevance.*

CHAPTER 2

AI & LAW: LEGAL STORYTELLING

Key briefing points about this essay:

- Some attorneys are trained to do just-the-facts legal arguments
- Only recently has such training also encompassed the skills of legal storytelling
- Composing and conveying a sufficient legal story can make or break a legal case
- Lawyers often do not have the inclination nor time to put together such stories
- Into this void comes the use of AI-based legal storytelling apps

Introduction

Have a quick legally minded quiz for you.

Which will best win a legal case, the use of a set of stark legal arguments or a compelling legal story that encompasses and enlivens those legal arguments?

I'm sure that attorneys seeking just-the-facts kind of legal tussles would exclaim that the use of unadorned legal arguments is by far the most judicious approach. The thing is, it is somewhat rare that a laundry list of legal arguments alone carries the day. Instead, an articulate and persuasive legal story that contains those legal arguments is often a more assured winner.

Welcome to the world of legal storytelling.

As you know, legal storytelling takes place both within and outside of the courtroom. Attorneys are called upon to tell legal stories in oral exhortations and also in everyday written form. One minute, you are explicating a legal story while standing in court during a trial, and the next you are elucidating a legal story to your client or fellow colleagues while conferring privately at your law office. The myriad of legal correspondences that you compose and send is akin to telling a story, sometimes in lengthy prose and in other cases in a shorter legal lingo format.

Per the *Michigan Bar Journal*, the importance of legal storytelling cannot be overstated: "Storytelling has many legal applications. Practicing law is grounded in the ability to communicate effectively. Stories are an excellent way to focus and direct thought. The most successful trial lawyers are storytellers, who use stories to create a connection with their audiences" (article by Heather Simmons, August 2015).

This idea of lawyers telling stories might seem somewhat obvious, but in the pell-mell rush of day-to-day legal wrangling, there tends to be a focus on *legal arguments* more so than legal storytelling.

In other words, the baseline assumption by attorneys is that a dutifully professed legal argument is what will win the day rather than some kind of puffy embellished story per se. The problem though is that a legal argument could go in one ear and come out the other. For jurors, a powerful legal argument by a legally steeped attorney might seem exceedingly dry and overly hard to follow. Meanwhile, a much less legally cohesive argument that is emboldened in a legally apt and compelling story might be much more readily understood and accepted by a jury.

Be forewarned that you skirt the need for suitable legal storytelling at your own peril (and that of your clients, presumably so).

Despite the strong case to be made for appropriately and reliably undertaking legal storytelling, many lawyers are still resistant to the notion overall. Perhaps in law school, they were taught to stridently strip away the presumed nonsense and noise surrounding legal arguments and get directly to the legally pertinent points. Sure, that might be handy when among fellow attorneys, but this might not be nearly as effective when communicating with clients, jurors, and nor even with judges (yes, judges too have been shown to be influenced by legal storytelling).

Another likely concern with legal storytelling is the use of the word "story" itself. If you are spotted telling a story, it is conceivable that others will immediately believe that you are making things up. We all tend to construe that a story or the act of storytelling is part fiction and part fact. You might face the danger that your storytelling is turned against you, namely that the listener or reader will mentally get trapped into suspiciousness about the legal arguments due to being wrapped within a story.

An article by Maureen Collins in the *Illinois Bar Journal* recounts these kinds of qualms that seem to go part and parcel with legal storytelling: "There are negative connotations as well. Some lawyers tell 'stories' rather than telling the truth. These oversimplifications ignore the very nature of what we do as advocates: tell our client's story intertwined with the law in such a way as to convince the 'listener,' be it judge or jury, that our client is in the right" (in "Lawyer As Storyteller" of the *Illinois Bar Journal*, 2000).

The overarching point is that legal storytelling is simultaneously alluring and yet also potentially filled with pitfalls. Relating a legal story is not always a bed of roses. Be careful in crafting legal stories and in proffering them.

I dare to emphasize that the potential risks or downsides should not be an excuse to forego legal storytelling all told. That would seem to be the proverbial head-in-the-sand strategy and unlikely to be fruitful in the long run of any venerated legal career.

AI Heroically Rides Into Legal Storytelling

Let's shift gears and bring someone else, or actually something else, into this whole legal storytelling tale. We need to bring to the legal theatre the use of AI in the storytelling realm. Various AI techniques and technologies can be utilized as a means for constructing legal stories, along with deconstructing them too.

Briefly, you undoubtedly already are familiar with Natural Language Processing (NLP), such as the likes of Alexa and Siri. This kind of AI capability can be used to piece together a legal story. In a similar but reverse manner, AI can be used to deconstruct a legal story.

Assume that you have sketched out the legal arguments for a particular case. You want to make this into a coherent and engaging legal story. Some attorneys are clueless about converting from legal stuffiness into an apt legal story. An AI system devised for such conversion or transformation takes as input the legal arguments and attempts to produce a legal story for your review and editing.

The other direction is possible too. You can input a legal story, and the AI will try to extract out the embodied legal arguments. This can be handy for an attorney that might want an alternative way of scrutinizing a lengthy legal narrative that an opposing attorney has provided in a briefing. By looking at the AI-generated extraction, you can mull over what you found by your own inspection of the legal story and see if the extraction matches (perhaps you missed an argument here or there).

As might be readily apparent, these kinds of AI legal story-producing and AI extraction programs are currently aimed at aiding human lawyers. In theory, assuming that we someday attain semi-autonomous or fully autonomous AI-based legal reasoning, it is conceivable that the AI will directly communicate such legal stories to key stakeholders such as the judge, jurors, clients, etc.

Conclusion

No need to worry right now about AI that goes over your head and tells a better legal story than you can. We aren't anywhere close to that as yet.

Time to brush up on your legal storytelling skills, including the potential for seeking some legal storytelling advice or assistance via your handy-dandy AI-based legal storyteller app.

.

Note: *For supplemental materials depicting the aspects discussed in this chapter, refer to Appendix B, which contains various augmented diagrams, charts, and additional related facets of relevance*

CHAPTER 3
AI & LAW:
LAWYER GENERALISTS

Key briefing points about this essay:

- A thorny question for attorneys consists of whether to specialize or not
- There are a variety of legal specializations to choose from
- Some say it is better to remain as a generalized legal practitioner of the law
- There are numerous tradeoffs to consider
- One surprising factor involves the emergence of AI in the law

Introduction

Sometimes choices make for headaches, though a bona fide case can be made that having a multitude of choices can also be salvation and a welcomed way ahead. In this particular case, I am referring to the choices that budding attorneys have regarding selecting a legal specialization. There are many legal specializations available.

The topmost choice though would be whether to even pursue a legal specialization at all. Maybe it is wiser to be a general legal practitioner rather than hanging your hat on a specific legal niche.

This perplexing choice is often angst-ridden.

Perhaps you can make more money as a legal specialist. Your career might blossom by taking on a particular legal specialty and then aim to become highly ranked as world-class in that niche. There are lots of advantages to picking a legal specialization.

As an example of the more "notable" specializations, the State Bar of California certifies legal specialists in these areas of the law:

- Admiralty and Maritime Law
- Appellate Law
- Bankruptcy Law
- Criminal Law
- Estate Planning, Trust and Probate Law
- Family Law
- Franchise and Distribution Law
- Immigration and Nationality Law
- Legal Malpractice Law
- Taxation Law
- Workers' Compensation Law

Think of the excitement about opting to become well-known as the best in one of those categories. You can focus all your legal acumen on just one major topic. No need to try and straddle across a multitude of legal areas. Just stick to your knitting, as they say.

But wait for a second, there are logically sound reasons to not choose a legal specialization.

Suppose you pick a particular specialty and it turns out you don't especially like that area of the law. Oops, you've put your eggs into one basket. It can become your personal legal career anchor. Once you've made the move into that legal subfield, you could be labeled with it for life. No turning back.

Perhaps equally unattractive would be that the legal specialty dries up. Maybe the number and variety of clients seeking legal services in that subfield slows down and becomes a mere trickle. Now, in this admittedly gloomy scenario, you are going toe to toe with other hungry lawyers vying for the dwindling supply of money-paying clients.

The dog-eat-dog world is at your legal doorstep. This could impact your livelihood, including putting you out of work.

A better approach might be to remain as a general practitioner of the law. You can be ready to swing into a legal specialty down the road if the right opportunity presents itself. Don't get pinned down too early. Keep your options open. See how the subfields are faring and then make a reasoned and safer choice.

Of course, the legal specialist might contend that the general practitioner that belatedly tries to shove their way into a specialty has missed the boat. By the time the new entrant ultimately gets fully up-to-speed, those that earlier selected the particular subfield will have long passed them. In a sense, the latecomer will never catch up.

And so on the exasperating debate rumbles around in the heads of most lawyers.

Sure, some lawyers in their heart of hearts know beforehand the exact specialty that they want to practice. Some dreamed of attaining that specific legal specialty. For them, the choice was easy or somehow magically preordained. Good for them, we might all applaud, but not every burgeoning lawyer has that divined inspiration upon going into law school.

There might be another factor that could come to play in this conundrum about whether to specialize in the law or remain generalized. It is a factor that catches some attorneys by surprise since they haven't usually had the topic at the top of their minds on this legal career aching issue.

I'm talking about AI as an emerging factor in the specialization versus generalization gambit.

You see, AI is gradually becoming infused into the legal field. AI-based legal reasoning capabilities are increasingly getting better and aiding those that embrace AI-infused LegalTech. This is demonstrably a stellar trend and will get stronger over time.

AI Is A Sound Factor To Be Heard

How in the world does AI in the law have anything to do with attorneys picking a legal specialty over being a general practitioner of the law?

First, consider the overall societal and legislative trend that seems to be generating more and more laws, which in turn would seem to bolster the drive toward legal specializations: "At the same time, legislatures continue to pass new legislation, more often to modify or amend rather than supersede existing legislation. Because lawyers must keep abreast of both judicial and legislative developments, it follows that lawyers will tend to increasingly narrow their scope of expertise, particularly as the returns to specialization increase" (according to the University of Toronto legal scholars Benjamin Alarie, Anthony Niblett, and Albert Yoon in their paper "How Artificial Intelligence Will Affect the Practice of Law").

Your initial reaction would likely be that this surely indicates that specializations are the preferred avenue over remaining as a general practitioner. Well, that might not exactly be the case.

The advent of AI-based capabilities in the law might reduce the value of being specialized due to the AI being able to provide any lawyer with the specialized legal acumen at the touch of a button. In that sense, specializations are a dime a dozen. All you need to do is access an AI-based legal specialization tool and a generalized practitioner is armed equally as a human attorney that has spent their entire career on that specific focus.

That kind of sounds like a dig against those that opt to go into a legal specialization. Not necessarily.

What could happen is that AI can aid legal specialists in branching out, as per the insights of these legal researchers: "Lawyers may be able to broaden rather than narrow their areas of specialization. Unshackled from the daunting task of reading a growing corpus of materials, lawyers can use artificial intelligence to maintain areas of expertise and develop new ones."

Yes, it appears as though AI giveth and taketh away when it comes to the specialization versus generalization question for legal beagles. The emergence of AI in the law could undercut the deepness of an attorney in a specialty, and meanwhile, spur the specialist to become essentially a specialist in a multitude of legal niches.

Conclusion

You'll have to decide whether the AI factor makes a difference in your own career path. The odds are that anyone in law school right now is not yet under the gun in terms of changes due to AI. The AI factor will more likely surface for those that are say young teens in middle school today and that later on in life expect to become lawyers.

May AI be of aid to them in the future and not ostensibly dissuade them from pursuing a rewarding career as an attorney.

Note: *For supplemental materials depicting the aspects discussed in this chapter, refer to Appendix B, which contains various augmented diagrams, charts, and additional related facets of relevance.*

CHAPTER 4

AI & LAW: NP EQUALS P QUESTION

Key briefing points about this essay:

- There is an important open question in the computer science field worth pondering
- Simply stated, the question is whether NP equals P (NP=P?)
- Turns out that is a quite difficult problem to answer
- If we knew the answer it would make a big difference for AI
- And would make a big difference for the use of AI in the law

Introduction

Fame awaits you!

Most lawyers would likely welcome becoming world-famous. In that case, I can proffer a suggestion of how to gain global acclaim. Furthermore, this would be enduring fame. I dare say you would likely be handed a Nobel Prize and your name would be enshrined in the history books.

There is just one small catch.

Your fame would be due to having solved a vexing and seemingly unsolvable computer science question, rather than as a result of your acumen as a barrister. Sorry about that, but heck, fame is fame.

The way to gain that kind of fame would be to solve an extremely perplexing question that is well-known and well-puzzling to all purist computer scientists. Get yourself ready for the question.

Is NP = P?

That's it.

The question is usually phrased as "NP = ?P" so as to emphasize that it is a question and not somehow misunderstood as an assertive fact.

Nobody can say for sure whether NP is equal to P. You are welcome to provide a bona fide and irrefutable proof that NP does equal to P, or if you prefer then showcase the alternative, which is that NP does not equal to P. Either way is fine.

By now, you are probably scratching your head and wondering what in the blazes is NP and what is P, and why do we care whether they are equal to each other or not.

Let's unpack the matter. In addition, you'll gradually see that this is a question pertinent to computer science all told, which then also encompasses the application of AI to the law. In short, since AI technology is based on computers, and since the act of computing revolves around the NP equaling P question, it is logically deducible that the efforts to construct and use AI for legal reasoning are subject to the same provisions.

The Devil Is In The Details

I'll briefly explain the NP and P particulars.

For any readers that are computer scientists, I apologize in advance that I will be mightily simplifying the matters at hand. This is due to the constraints of trying to explain a quite complex matter in such an abbreviated manner to non-computer scientists, seeking to convey just the overarching essence.

Thanks for your bearing with me on this.

Now then, the field of computer science includes a subfield generally labeled as computational complexity theory.

You can think of computational complexity as a means of trying to ascertain how fast or how many steps it will take for a computer to solve a given problem. If it would take a computer a million years to crank through and produce a solution, we might reasonably say that the problem is not in any practical way feasibly solved via a computer. Yes, a solution by the computational crunching is apparently ultimately findable, but we would all be dead and gone long before the computer rings a bell to report the result.

One facet to also consider is whether the final result produced is indeed a correct solution and not some erroneous outcome. Thus, we would also want to have a ready means to verify that the proffered solution is correct.

It can oftentimes be seemingly easy to verify a result, whilst the effort to produce the result was tremendous and extremely extensive. Imagine that you are given a thousand numbers that are both positive and negative in value, and asked to find the two such numbers that add exactly to zero. It could take a long time to find the two such numbers. To verify that the two numbers do add to zero would be child's play, namely that you would just add the claimed two found numbers and be able to immediately verify or invalidate the declared result.

A computer program can be construed as an implementation of some stated algorithm. I mention this because the best way to mull over the computational complexity aspects is to keep in your mind that a computer is running a program that is an instantiation of an algorithm. The algorithm is the envisioned or described steps needed to solve a problem at hand.

Okay, so pretend that we make a category that contains all computer solvable problems. Within that category, we focus on the ones that are relatively easy to verify as to the results that are produced.

Of those problems, subdivide them as follow: Which ones take a long time or potentially incur a heck of a lot of steps to solve (we'll call those NP), and which ones are relatively fast or take a lot fewer steps to solve (we'll call those P)?

More formally, P is defined as: "P (deterministic Polynomial time) is the class of decision problems that are algorithmically solved in polynomial time" (per the handy article by Kazimierz Trzesicki, "Can AI Be Intelligent?" in the *Studies In Logic, Grammar, And Rhetoric*, 2016). And NP can be defined as: "NP (Non-deterministic Polynomial-time) is the class of decision problems solvable in polynomial time by a theoretical non-deterministic Turing Machine (TM). It consists of those problems which can be correctly decided by some computation of a non-deterministic TM in a number of steps which is a polynomial function of the size of its input."

The key here is that the problems that we wish to solve via computers of an NP nature are problematic because the larger the given problem becomes the longer and longer it will take to have the computer generate a solution (e.g., the traveling salesman problem, the factoring of prime numbers). This is much more convoluted and bloated (intractable) than the problems of a P nature.

Some believe that perhaps the NP classified problems can be "reduced" to being P problems, such that if we are clever enough, we can find a foolproof way to convert or transform NP-oriented algorithms into P-oriented algorithms.

If so, it means that we can readily use computers to pragmatically solve those otherwise seemingly thorny and computationally intractable NP problems.

I ask you then to find a robust and unassailable mathematical proof that can showcase the open matter of whether NP equals P.

By your doing so, you will win the hearts of computer scientists, mathematicians, and many others. Plus, you will indubitably be hailed and revered across the globe and throughout history for your brilliance and ability to solve one of the most vexing questions of our times.

Yes or no, does NP = P?

Answering that question will also aid in the advent of applying AI into the field of law. If you proved that NP does equal P, there are likely new doors that would open for advances in AI that could practically and dutifully be keenly used for AI-based legal reasoning due to the boosted computational tractability.

Conclusion

You see, the fame about this would ostensibly spill over into the legal domain and therefore you would be acclaimed by all, including your fellow legal professionals and those that devoutly practice law.

Good luck, and please get started on this right away.

Note: *For supplemental materials depicting the aspects discussed in this chapter, refer to Appendix B, which contains various augmented diagrams, charts, and additional related facets of relevance.*

CHAPTER 5

AI & LAW: IF-THEN CORNERSTONE

Key briefing points about this essay:

- The use of If-Then statements is a cornerstone underlying the history of law
- Most famous perhaps is the code of laws established by Hammurabi
- During the initial days of applying AI to the law, If-Then was king
- The If-Then fell out of favor and gave way to machine learning techniques
- If-Then revival is underway and typified by the common-sense atlas of ATOMIC

Introduction

Take a quiet and reflective moment to reflect upon the all-powerful If-Then statement.

How did that go?

If you aren't sure what this If-Then hubbub is all about then please do keep reading.

Ample evidence of the utility associated with If-Then statements can be readily traced to the earliest of formalized legal rules. Consider for example the famous legal regulations proclaimed by Hammurabi during his reign as the king of Babylon in the years 1792 to 1750 B.C. The rather succinct collection of his two hundred eighty-two legal rules stood looming over the public per a massive stone pillar upon which the Hammurabi code of laws was carved upon (written in cuneiform chiseled script).

Here's one of those laws: *If a man put out the eye of another man then his eye shall be put out.*

That seems like a relatively straightforward law. We generally associate this particular legal rule with the even simpler "eye for an eye" provision, which is well-known among those versed in the legal profession as the doctrine of *lex talionis* (laws of retribution).

For those of you that have visited the U.S. Supreme Court, you've undoubtedly noticed that the south wall of the venerated courtroom showcases marble carvings of Hammurabi. His pioneering approach to the casting of laws is still among us to this very day. Some would say that it is partially due to the simplicity and transparency of his code of laws, namely that he used a series of straight-out If-Then statements.

I'll share with you another one of his laws: *If a man knocks out the teeth of his equal then his teeth shall be knocked out.*

You might have noticed that this law seems quite similar to the eye for an eye law.

One supposes that this other law could be construed as a tooth for a tooth stipulation. But you would seemingly assume that if the eye for an eye was of a generalized nature, there is no specific need for a tooth for a tooth rule too. The tooth for a tooth ought to be subsumed under the eye for an eye law.

In fact, upon seeing the tooth for a tooth provision, you might be tempted to rethink the eye for an eye rule. Perhaps the If-Then statement about the retribution associated with eyes is exclusively about eyes and does not apply to other parts of the body. Furthermore, the If-Then encompassing an eye for an eye is not apparently intended as a broader generalization all told (we would have assumed that it meant that any taking of one kind shall be met with a like taking).

This raises a number of interesting questions about the structure and interpretation of If-Then statements that come within the legal realm. Should an If-Then be strictly construed or can it be claimed as more open-ended and wider in meaning? If multiple If-Then statements pertain to each other, can we gauge their meaning in isolation, or do we have to consider them rightfully as a collective?

And so on.

AI And The Return Of If-Then Statements

Let's shift gears and talk about computers in the law, especially the advent of AI capabilities for legal purposes.

When the initial attempts were made to transform laws into computer programming code, the belief was that the effort would be entirely quick and easy to accomplish. The thinking was that since laws are ostensibly If-Then statements, the writing of those laws as programs would be easy-peasy. All you need to do is take a given law, rewrite it using the stated syntax for a chosen programming language, and you would voila produce a computer-usable version of those text-based laws.

This same notion was further accelerated by the early days of AI that involved the rise of expert systems or oftentimes referred to as rules-based systems. At the time, many domains were being reduced to If-Then types of constructs, such as medicine and the undertaking of medical diagnoses. Tools to build expert systems allowed easy entry of If-Then statements. The law became a hoped-for realm that was presumed as being fully and naturally amendable to hand-coding into If-Then rules for use within a rules-based system software package.

As you might be aware, the use of expert systems gradually tailed off. There are numerous reasons why this hot trend cooled down. One such drawback is illustrated by the eye for an eye and the tooth for a tooth conundrum. It was vexing to try and interconnect If-Then statements, and eventually, some larger efforts became a morass of conflicting and confounding If-Then rules.

Do not though write an epitaph for the If-Then.

Some believe that the If-Then deserves a second chance.

For example, a large-scale effort to create a database that can be used as an AI semblance of common-sense reasoning has opted to focus on using If-Then statements. This is a departure from the conventional approach to infusing common sense into a machine-like programming language (the typical method involves devising concepts and facts as part of an elaborate data network).

Researchers at the University of Washington and the Allen Institute for Artificial Intelligence are building a common-sense atlas via the use of If-Then statements: "We present ATOMIC, an atlas of everyday commonsense reasoning, organized through 877,000 textual descriptions of inferential knowledge. Compared to existing resources that center around taxonomic knowledge, ATOMIC focuses on inferential knowledge organized as typed if-then relations with variables (e.g., 'if X pays Y a compliment, then Y will likely return the compliment')." This is ongoing research and described in summary detail via a paper entitled "ATOMIC: An Atlas of Machine Commonsense for If-Then Reasoning" as posted in the Cornell University arXiv repository.

This revival of the If-Then provides impetus to consider bringing back the If-Then as a part of today's AI in the law endeavors. Whereas other AI methods have taken center stage (such as machine learning and deep neural networks), we ought to not turn our backs on the still viable If-Then statement.

Conclusion

By taking a hybrid approach of using If-Then and cojoining with other AI methods, we are decidedly going to have better luck in the tortuous path toward devising AI-based legal reasoning and achieving the lofty aspiration of lawyering by computers that are on par with human attorneys.

A final If-Then for now: *If we ultimately reach a lawyer-in-a-box goal then we'll seemingly thank Hammurabi for his cornerstone work on those ubiquitous If-Then legal rules.*

Note: *For supplemental materials depicting the aspects discussed in this chapter, refer to Appendix B, which contains various augmented diagrams, charts, and additional related facets of relevance.*

CHAPTER 6

AI & LAW: LEGAL BANS ON AI

Key briefing points about this essay:

- Recent clamor indicates increasing pressures to ban AI in various respects
- All out bans on AI are rarer and generally untenable
- The United Nations has gotten onto the ban AI bandwagon
- You can expect a need for lawyers versed in legal elements of AI to be highly sought
- Some will aid in crafting new regulations, others will aid firms deploying AI, etc.

Introduction

The excitement and unabashed love for AI have lost a lot of its allure. Stakeholders across all boundaries are beseeching the emergence of AI that is rotten and causing a slew of inequities.

Out of this muck has arisen an emboldened cry to ban AI.

That's a headline-grabbing refrain by those that believe fervently that the downsides of today's AI systems are so foul that we'd all be better off without AI. In just the last few years we've gone from a kind of glowing embrace of AI to becoming sternly wary of AI.

The proclaimed *AI For Good* that permeated the unbridled rush toward AI has finally shifted toward the condemnation of *AI For Bad.*

The ban envisioned would be a legal banishment.

An expressed need to legally ban AI in various respects has arisen at all levels, including by the UN human rights chief Ms. Michelle Bachelet. Per the reporting by *UN News*: "Urgent action is needed as it can take time to assess and address the serious risks this technology poses to human rights, warned the High Commissioner: 'The higher the risk for human rights, the stricter the legal requirements for the use of AI technology should be'. Ms. Bachelet also called for AI applications that cannot be used in compliance with international human rights law, to be banned" (as indicated in "Urgent Action Needed Over Artificial Intelligence Risks To Human Rights" United Nations *UN News*).

Of course, outright wholescale banning of AI is not exactly what is intended.

The general notion entails putting in place laws that make certain aspects or uses of AI legally viable and pre-approved, while other aspects or particularly untoward uses would be legally banned. This assuredly sounds sensible. Keep producing the good and beneficial outcomes that flow from AI. We want that and welcome it. Meanwhile, restrict or entirely prohibit the bad uses of AI.

Turns out that this desire to promote and simultaneously prevent the advent of particular AI aspects is a lot harder to bring to reality than it might seem on the surface. Sorry to say that it isn't like there are two spigots of cold water and hot water, whereby you simply turn on one and turn off the other. That's not how AI works.

AI Needs Some Lawful Governing

I've frequently indicated that there are two ways to conceive of AI in the law.

One is to be attentive to the application of AI to legal efforts.

For example, making use of AI-based Natural Language Processing (NLP) that is able to analyze legal contracts and aid in crafting and interpreting the contents of a contract. Another application of AI to the law entails using AI during e-Discovery. Rather than by hand trying to sort through thousands of online pages of discovery documents, you can use various AI tools to do the laborious screening for you.

The other overarching way to intertwine AI and the law consists of the legal means for governing AI.

This brings up the question of whether our existing laws are strong enough to encompass the governance of AI systems and their development. Many assert that our prevailing laws are insufficient and exasperatingly allow the *AI For Bad* to arise without any legal constraints or legal repercussions.

You might recall that a few years ago there was a vocal call for new regulations to deal with advances in facial recognition. Indeed, a variety of local, state, federal, and international laws were enacted to try and reign in the Big Brother concerns about how facial recognition was being rolled out. A stoking factor was that the AI facial recognition software tended to be faulty, encompassing false positives and false negatives that were especially egregious by race and gender factors.

In more recent times, this call by the UN High Commissioner for an AI ban was based on extensive current-day analysis by her office.

A wide array of AI uses were identified as extraordinarily disconcerting: "There are several sectors where the use of those AI systems is particularly concerning, according to the report. They include law enforcement, where algorithms may influence a decision to arrest a criminal, as well as public services, where AI models can help determine welfare entitlements all the way to whether a family should be flagged for visits by childcare services. In the workplace, the report pointed to the risk of using algorithms to monitor and manage workers. And online, AI systems can be used to support content management decisions, which is instrumental in deciding the type of content that each user is exposed to" (as indicated in "AI: Ban The Algorithms That Threaten Our Human Rights Says UN Chief" by Daphine Leprince-Ringuet, *ZDNet*).

Lawyers are going to be needed on all sides of this AI banning issue.

First, lawyers versed in the nuances of regulating AI will be needed to help in crafting the envisioned new laws. There are thorny legal questions to be dealt with. How do you properly define AI within a regulatory framework? If the AI definition is overly narrow, the bad uses might insidiously sneak through. If the AI definition is overly broad, the AI that is devised for good might inadvertently get blocked or ensnared.

Second, once these new laws that ban AI are on the books, you can bet that there will be legal cases aplenty. Lawyers that know about the intricacies of AI will be sought by software vendors that are dragged into court due to accusations of violating said laws. AI-aware defense lawyers will be in demand. AI-aware prosecutors will be in demand.

Third, companies that make or release AI software will seek to protect themselves from legal exposures underlying the new regulations that ban certain types of uses of AI. You can assume that in-house legal counsels will beef up on their AI legal prowess. Likewise, law firms proffering legal services associated with AI bans will be called upon to assist companies that have seemingly strayed from the regulatory provisions.

Conclusion

It would be folly to ban all of AI. Besides the near impossibility of tightly defining what is being banned, the AI spigot all told would be greatly diminished and the goodness of what AI can offer to society would be effectively shut down.

We will instead be better off by selectively indicating what types of AI or uses of AI should be considered banned. Admittedly, this is a fine line and not going to be easily nailed down. That's why we assuredly require AI-savvy attorneys to enter into this technology good versus bad regulatory battle.

One might somewhat cynically state that the *AI For Bad* is stoking demand for lawyers that are up-to-speed about AI, for which the billable hours spigot is going to be turned wide open.

Note: *For supplemental materials depicting the aspects discussed in this chapter, refer to Appendix B, which contains various augmented diagrams, charts, and additional related facets of relevance.*

CHAPTER 7

AI & LAW:
AI BILL OF RIGHTS

Key briefing points about this essay:

- A cornerstone of our existent laws and society is embodied in the U.S. Bill of Rights
- Lawyers are versed in the nuances of the Bill of Rights
- Today's spreading of AI is worrisome that our basic rights are being violated
- Some suggest that we need an augmented AI-oriented bill of rights
- Such an effort is underway by the White House Office of Science and Technology Policy (OSTP)

Introduction

Part and parcel of being a lawyer would seem to also include a great familiarity with the Bill of Rights. This is hammered home during law school. While practicing law, the odds are that on a daily basis you refer to or somehow reflect upon the revered and venerated Bill of Rights.

Imagine where we might be without the Bill of Rights.

Yikes!

Presumably, there would be a lack of guarantees pertaining to our personal freedoms and our overarching rights as individuals. The government's powers for adjudication and akin proceedings might be unchecked, leading possibly to morally offensive abuses upon the general public. And so on.

The Bill of Rights is pretty much inarguably a cornerstone of our society. Over the years since the Bill of Rights was first adopted, numerous U.S. Supreme Court rulings have aided in dealing with open-ended questions regarding the full meaning of the words presented therein. In addition, you could readily assert that those founding words have been interpreted and reapplied to modern-day issues, keeping them fresh and enlivened despite dating back to their ratification on December 15, 1791.

None of this is particularly surprising or newsworthy to lawyers per se. The aforementioned importance of the Bill of Rights and the ongoing legal efforts to keep the revered passages up-to-date is abundantly known by attorneys and considered an obvious and necessary part of practicing law.

Why have I dragged you through the storied history of the Bill of Rights?

Because there are some that believe we need an entirely additional and newly minted bill of rights. To clarify, this does not suggest that we must undo or replace the existing Bill of Rights. Instead, this new bill of rights would seemingly sit astride the "old" Bill of Rights and provide crucially needed updates and focus that the ongoing and traditional Bill of Rights ostensibly lacks.

You see, there are those that contend we need an AI bill of rights, as it were.

Actually, this might be better phrased as an AI-oriented bill of rights or perhaps an AI-safety bill of rights, such that the devised rights would confer special *limitations* upon AI and also provide special and vital *protections* for humanoids from the evildoing of AI.

Whether this is a brilliant idea and deserves incredible accolades, or whether this is a somewhat misplaced notion and ought to be summarily dropped, you can decide for yourself. The point is that there is quite a mixed reaction to the proposed possibility of crafting yet another bill of rights. Are you serious, ask incredulously some attorneys? Other lawyers might breathe a sigh of relief and exhort that this is something stridently needed and we ought to get to the task straight away.

Turning Up The Heat On AI Inequities

Rest assured that this matter is not one of lighthearted folly.

The existing White House Office of Science and Technology Policy (OSTP) is in the process of floating the contention that an AI bill of rights is sorely needed. Here is their devout reasoning: "Soon after ratifying our Constitution, Americans adopted a Bill of Rights to guard against the powerful government we had just created—enumerating guarantees such as freedom of expression and assembly, rights to due process and fair trials, and protection against unreasonable search and seizure. Throughout our history, we have had to reinterpret, reaffirm, and periodically expand these rights. In the 21st century, we need a "bill of rights" to guard against the powerful technologies we have created" (as stated by the OSTP Director Eric Lander and OSTP Deputy Director Alondra Nelson in "Americans Need A Bill Of Rights For An AI-Powered World," *Wired*, October 8, 2021).

They explain that these are the kinds of rights infringement issues that such an added bill of rights would deal with: "Our country should clarify the rights and freedoms we expect data-driven technologies to respect. What exactly those are will require discussion, but here are some possibilities: your right to know when and how AI is influencing a decision that affects your civil rights and civil liberties; your freedom from being subjected to AI that hasn't been carefully audited to ensure that it's accurate, unbiased, and has been trained on sufficiently representative data sets; your freedom from pervasive or discriminatory surveillance and monitoring in your home, community, and workplace; and your right to meaningful recourse if the use of an algorithm harms you."

Outreach to the general public by OSTP has gotten underway, seeking public requests for information as sought for input into the considerations involved. This effort aims to draft an augmented AI-coping set of rights at a somewhat record pace: "In the coming months, the White House Office of Science and Technology Policy (which we lead) will be developing such a bill of rights, working with partners and experts across the federal government, in academia, civil society, the private sector, and communities all over the country."

One way to implement this "bill of rights" has been postulated as requiring federal contractors to adhere to the provisions or else suffer adverse consequences accordingly. Another would be that the federal government would only purchase technologies that fully abided by the "bill of rights" stipulations. The assumption is that the states might opt to similarly adopt the same posture.

There is a realization that this is likely to simply be a hyphenated form of rights and that perhaps should be expressed in quotes as a "bill of rights" that is decidedly not of the same magnitude as the actual Bill of Rights. Indeed, some worry that even referring to the proposed semi-regulatory provisions as a bill of rights is confusing and problematic. Steer clear of this, they argue. The counterargument is that by invoking the famous weightiness of the Bill of Rights that the significance of this matter will rise to the prominence that it deserves.

Conclusion

You can easily find lots of divergent opinions about this AI-focused bill of rights pursuit.

Some insist that the existing Bill of Rights is entirely satisfactory and trying to spawn or tailgate off them with an additional document is legally and societally questionable. We might end up with a legal scramble as numerous legal wrangling's try to square the true Bill of Rights with the son-of or daughter-of bill of rights.

One thing that seems clear-cut, the whole matter will likely generate a lot of lawyering hours and be the next big thing on the dockets of our courts, so hopefully, the benefits will be worth the inherent costs thereof.

Note: *For supplemental materials depicting the aspects discussed in this chapter, refer to Appendix B, which contains various augmented diagrams, charts, and additional related facets of relevance.*

CHAPTER 8
AI & LAW: AUTONOMOUS AI BANS

Key briefing points about this essay:

- AI has gotten into trouble and transcended the initial professed welcoming
- We have discovered that AI systems can embed all kinds of unsavory aspects
- Debates about what type of AI should be legally banned is an ongoing exercise
- It might seem obvious that a legal ban on AI for autonomous weapons should occur
- A close look at the autonomous weapons issue showcases tradeoffs exist even there

Introduction

Ban that darned AI.

That is the rallying cry for many that have become fed up with the foul deeds being performed by some AI systems. Perhaps the most prominent such proclamation of recent note entails the use of AI-based facial recognition systems.

Whereas the original assumption was that facial recognition would be a quite handy form of technology, the seedy underbelly of this particular kind of AI-infused high-tech was soon revealed. Turns out that the software tended at times to embed various racial and gender-related biases. Some attributed this to the nature of the AI developers that put together this kind of tech. Others pointed out that the data used to train the Machine Learning algorithms contained intrinsic biases that got carried over into the everyday functioning of the facial recognition systems.

In any case, a variety of legally imposed bans were quickly enacted. Some of the bans were extremely restrictive and nearly choked off any commercial use of facial recognition in predefined circumstances. Meanwhile, other bans were much milder. The mildest bans were accused of being so watered down that they essentially carried no legally useful weight at all.

Part of the problem with imposing a ban on AI-related tech is that there are two sides to the considerations involved. The obvious side is to use a ban to prevent abusive applications of the technology. If you turn the coin over, the other side indicates that there are lots of fruitful and notably beneficial uses, for which the legally imposed bans can end up squelching.

There is a fine line that needs to be observed about imposing legal bans on AI. Somehow, there must be sufficient latitude to allow for so-called *AI For Good* to arise, and yet still be able to catch and hopefully prevent the lamented *AI For Bad* from being let loose.

You might be tempted to believe that the case of AI-based facial recognition is ostensibly an obvious instance of the tug of war between promoting AI innovations and preventing AI evildoings. Even a casual glance at what is at stake would make apparent that we want some semblance of facial recognition for our ease in daily living. And of course, we don't want Big Brother or similar disadvantages that can accrue from facial recognition.

Perhaps we need to look at something involving AI that would earn seemingly unanimous agreement that a ban ought to be established. Specifically, let's consider the use of AI as the underlying key element for creating and deploying autonomous weapon systems.

AI And Autonomous Weapons On Trial

Surely, autonomous weapons systems would be decried as absolutely requiring a ban on the use of AI.

The idea would be that if AI was not allowed to be used in such weapons systems, those weapons would lose their capability to operate autonomously. Removing the AI ought to revert those weapons back into a human-based operational mode. Whether you favor or disfavor weapons, to begin with, at least the expunging of AI from the equation would keep us at a status quo of so-called conventional weaponry that requires a human-in-the-loop necessity.

In a research paper by legal scholars Kenneth Anderson and Matthew Waxman, the legal aspects of banning AI-powered autonomous weapons system is given close scrutiny (under the auspices of the *Columbia Law School*, Faculty Scholarship Publication entitled "Law and Ethics for Autonomous Weapon Systems: Why a Ban Won't Work and How the Laws of War Can"). There are plenty of international bans that have been proposed to deal with stopping the race toward autonomous weapons. As emphasized by these researchers: "The United States and its partners have grave interests -- legal, moral, and strategic -- in developing, simultaneously with new automated and autonomous weapons, a broadly shared normative framework and expectations for how these systems must perform to be lawful."

Let's briefly explore four crucial points made by the paper.

First, some would say that we could merely program the AI to be lawful in its use of any autonomous weapons.

Thus, rather than being worried about the AI fostering autonomous capacities, we harness the AI to make sure that such weaponry is only used in designated lawful ways. AI then controls AI, turning what might have been something unlawful into becoming fully lawful.

Few believe this would be a tried-and-true solution, as per this stated counterargument: "The first is a broad claim that machine programming will never reach the point of satisfying the fundamental ethical and legal principles required to field a lawful autonomous lethal weapon."

Secondly, perhaps we can rely upon morality rather than looking to the law per se: "The second major argument against development of autonomous weapon systems is a moral one: it is simply wrong per se to take the human moral agent entirely out of the firing loop." Of course, this morality perspective is not likely to prevent rogue actors from pursuing autonomous weapons. Furthermore, a case could be made that morality favors autonomous weapons since doing so could remove soldiers from the battlefield and seemingly reduce the loss of lives while at war.

Thirdly, from a wartime viewpoint, we traditionally assume that those engaged in combat can be held accountable for their actions. This is an internationally recognized legal facet. Of course, we tend to hold people accountable rather than holding "things" accountable, which raises a conundrum about the AI that empowers an autonomous weapon: "A third major argument holds that autonomous weapon systems that remove the human being from the firing loop are unacceptable because they undermine the possibility of holding anyone accountable for what, if done by a human soldier, might be a war crime." Some pointedly argue that those that either make the autonomous weapon or those that employ it are presumably people and ergo those are the people that could be held accountable.

The fourth consideration is that the availability of AI-based autonomous weapons will promote the urge to go to war since there is lessened harm or risk to human soldiers on the side that uses such weaponry.

The counterargument is that perhaps a semblance of mutually assured destruction via the AI infusion would serve as a disincentive and we would incur fewer wars accordingly.

Conclusion

As might be apparent, akin to the tradeoffs of banning AI high-tech such as facial recognition, the idea of banning AI that underlies even the starkly frightening advent of autonomous weapons systems has its similar legal conundrums at hand.

There seems to never be a free lunch, as it were, and banning AI is a sordid entanglement no matter what AI usage is bandied about.

Note: *For supplemental materials depicting the aspects discussed in this chapter, refer to Appendix B, which contains various augmented diagrams, charts, and additional related facets of relevance.*

CHAPTER 9

AI & LAW:
AI ROBO-ARTIST COPYRIGHTS

Key briefing points about this essay:

- There are plenty of copyright laws globally that serve to provide authorship protections
- Copyright goes to the creator of a novel work of art, music, literary narrative, etc.
- We naturally assume that a copyright can be held only by humans and not by non-humans
- Some ardently believe that AI ought to be permitted as a valid copyright holder
- Ongoing and strident legal debates on this are underway and not easily resolved

Introduction

Copyrights are pretty much an accepted legal form of expressive protection in nearly all countries across the globe (well, laws might vary quite a bit, but the core principle itself still seems relatively intact).

Whether you consider yourself to be an artist or not, suppose that you opt to compose a new musical score that is utterly novel, or you write a story that is in your own unique words, or maybe you splash some paint on a canvas and render a visually distinct work of art. These forms of artistry would appear to allow you the legal right to use copyright for the works that you've rendered.

Assuming that you are the genuine artist or author, the odds are that your ownership of that copyright will be relatively free and clear. There could be other complications such as whether your artistry perhaps violates someone else's prior copyright, but otherwise in the normal course of affairs, the copyright you hold will be considered legally binding and proper.

We all know that this form of Intellectual Property (IP) protection encompasses a myriad of forms such as artistic expressions, musical compositions, literary narratives, and the like. Furthermore, the creative work and its copyright will likely only last a designated amount of time. Most laws globally have a provision that the copyright will expire after a stated time period.

I realize that this indication about copyrights might seem rather ho-hum to any practicing attorney.

The twist to this seemingly mundane topic is the argument that the "you" in my earlier statement proffering that "you create a new work of art" could be equally replaced with the catchphrase of a so-called robo-artist or ostensibly with the more well-known moniker of Artificial Intelligence (AI).

Yes, there is a fervent debate taking place as to the open-ended claim that AI ought to be included as a copyright holder. The gist is that instead of having only a human being serving as a copyright holder, we would all summarily agree to anoint AI as a potential copyright holder too. In brief, an AI system that crafts a novel work of art, music, literary artifact, or any other salient material would legally be proclaimed as the author and ergo receive the IP credit and by law serve as the holder of the copyright.

Crazy talk, some are apt to vehemently exhort.

Absolutely makes sense, others exclaim in retort.

Entering Into The AI Copyright Holding Debacle

The most obvious basis for insisting that the AI should in fact be a copyright holder is the old adage that fair is fair. If an AI system has created an original work, the AI deserves the legally allowed reward for doing so, namely by bestowing the AI as the copyright holder. This plainly makes reasonable sense, the argument goes.

In other words, if a human-created an original work of some kind, there would be little bona fide debate that the human has earned the copyright entitlement (all else being equal). Thus, in all fairness, we should be willing to ensure that AI gets its deserved rights too. Anyone trying to suggest that a human in lieu of the AI should get the copyright is nefariously trying to strip the copyright from the proper holder and true artistic creator, as it were, and sordidly assign those legal rights to a false or inappropriate holder.

Sounds convincing, except for one gigantic flaw, so says the opposing viewpoint. The flaw is that today's AI is not sentient. This might come as a surprise since the general media oftentimes portrays existing AI as though it does possess a modicum of sentience. Do not be fooled. There isn't any AI as yet that comes even close to anything construed as sentience. That's a fact.

The inarguable fact that there isn't any AI of a sentient nature at this time would seem to settle the vitriolic discourse on whether AI ought to be legally permitted to hold a copyright. Until the day that AI crosses over into sentience, which we don't know when or if this will someday occur, the brash posture that AI can be a copyright holder would seem to be entirely and undisputedly mute.

Not necessarily, per the opinions of some that believe there is no preordained basis to set a requirement of sentience.

Where in existing copyright laws does the requirement exist that a copyright holder must be sentient? By and large, copyright laws usually merely indicate that the author of the work shall receive the copyright.

Numerous legal battles have tested the notion of authorship and the standing of purported copyright-seeking authors (this is often subsumed within the question of legal personhood for AI, which is either directly relevant or a sideshow tangent).

The famous or perhaps notably the infamous legal case of *Naruto v. David John Slater* that was decided in the Northern District of California entailed an attempt to prescribe copyright to a monkey named Naruto that for all practical purposes took by its own hands a series of photographic selfies. Plaintiffs argued vehemently that the crested macaque had independently and autonomously created the pictures. The court denied the copyright assignment and emphasized that a non-human such as an animal cannot be a copyright holder.

If a non-human cannot hold copyright, and if we are willing to agree that AI is not a human, we seem to reach the logically immutable conclusion that AI cannot hold a copyright.

Wait for a darned second, some bellow, if AI is or approaches sentience then we have to recalibrate our thinking and our laws to allow AI to serve as a copyright holder. Are we really going to be so restrictive and biased that we insist that only members of the human family can be authors and copyright owners?

A plethora of additional twists upon twists ensue.

For example, if a human programmed the AI, wouldn't we be denying the human their due if we declared that the AI alone was the copyright holder?

This brings up the messy notion of allowing for multiple copyright holders simultaneously for one work of art. As per the meaty discussion by researcher Jacopo Ciani about such arrangements: "Moreover, it is debated what 'arrangements' actually means, who made them (the person who built the core AI system, or the person who trained it?), how proximate the person and their 'arrangements' must be to the creation of the work and what does it happen if multiple contributors are involved in the development of the art-generating system" (as indicated in his fascinating paper entitled "Learning From Monkeys: Authorship Issues Arising From AI Technology").

All told, the preponderance of legal views at this time seems to suggest that we are prematurely wringing our hands about having AI serve as a copyright holder. The AI of today has not reached a seemingly needed hurdle to invoke such a crisis of copyright holding concerns. For now, the legal debate is worthy of early on discourse but would seem to be otherwise a preparatory exercise rather than a real-world assertion that robo-artists fully exist today.

Of course, a strong contingent continues to push that even today's AI is worthy of copyright holding. They would contend that the AI algorithms used currently are able to act "autonomously" and therefore sufficiently and independently arrive at human-like creations worthy of copyrights, sentient or not.

Conclusion

One even supposes that someday there might be AI of an adequate caliber that it too joins directly into the legally beefy argument, clamoring for the right of copyright, and we'll need to take a second look at the nature of copyright and the underlying laws that we might wish to adjust accordingly.

That is the proverbial sooner-or-later legal argument of the day.

Note: *For supplemental materials depicting the aspects discussed in this chapter, refer to Appendix B, which contains various augmented diagrams, charts, and additional related facets of relevance.*

CHAPTER 10

AI & LAW: ATTORNEY WORKLOADS

Key briefing points about this essay:

- Attorney workloads are notoriously high and at times bone crushing of mind and body
- On the surface, this seems fine as long as the hours are billable and making money
- Issues undercutting this include attorney burnout, heightened turnover, etc.
- AI and especially Machine Learning can be used to analyze attorney workloads
- Insights gleaned allow for workload balancing, plus spark use of AI-infused LegalTech

Introduction

If you are a practicing attorney, you undoubtedly also believe that you are overworked.

According to various workload surveys, this rather widespread claim and altogether bemoaning exhortation appears to be backed by actual data.

One recent study conducted by Bloomberg Law reported that law firm attorneys tended to average more than 54 hours per week of lawyering labor, while in-house attorneys were nearly in the same boat at around 51 hours per week. To clarify, those are merely averages. In that sense, the picture is even bleaker than it might otherwise seem. You see, it turns out that one-fifth of law firm lawyers indicated they at times were enduring 80 hours per week of nonstop barrister efforts and ended up with more than 100 hours per week in some instances.

Assuming that those were principally billable hours, there are outsiders that say that this seemingly constant drumbeat of excessive workload hours complaints is nothing more than crocodile tears. Be happy that you are working, the response goes. All those work hours are a blessing. You get to practice your legal craft, you are gainfully employed or kept in gear, and those long hours ought to be welcomed and cherished.

A standard retort is that the crushing workload takes a severe toll on the minds, bodies, and lives of lawyers. Per the survey, attorneys are apt to experience disrupted sleep patterns and be engulfed in heightened anxiety via the billable hour's excruciating treadmill. In addition, the Bureau of Labor Statistics indicates that there are serious health consequences that arise from lawyering overwork. The litany of concerns includes attorneys encountering caustic burnout, turning at times toward substance abuse, and generally embodying an oncoming drop in their sense of well-being.

A plethora of claimed fixes is proffered by proclaimed workload experts. These silver bullets include making sure to eat well and routinely practicing your mindfulness stress-reducing mantras. Sure, that can help and ought to be closely embraced. On the other hand, as long as those hours keep pounding away at you, some would decry those solutions as the classic proverb of merely moving around the chairs on the deck of the Titanic.

The core solution would seem to entail tackling the workload hours overload per se.

Into this dilemma steps a potential means of gauging and balancing the lawyering workloads, namely the use of AI. The notion is that AI can provide a possible one-two punch at coping with overbearing workloads. First, AI can be used to examine how hours are being consumed and potentially render balancing recommendations. Second, lawyers can leverage AI to aid in performing legal tasks, aiming to reduce the volume of human lawyering hours needed to complete given legal chores.

AI As A Tool For Workload Balancing

Let's go ahead and further unpack the ways that AI can serve as a tool for dealing with attorney overwork.

In busy law practice, there is often an inadequate effort undertaken to identify where the consumption of lawyering hours goes. Much of the judgment about the time being used is based on the seat of the pants conjecture. If a lawyer is working at the 80 or 100 hours per week mark, the assumption is that this is what must be required to sufficiently get the lawyering properly completed.

In short, despite boatloads of data being racked up by the painstaking logging of attorney hours, this treasure trove of data is singularly used for billing purposes. Little reflective thought goes into examining this same data to try and ascertain what is really occurring under the hood of the workload endeavors.

An emerging trend involves using AI techniques and technologies such as Machine Learning (ML) to computationally analyze the data and seek to find useful patterns therein. Are some attorneys taking on tasks that could be parceled out to fellow attorneys and balance the overall workloads accordingly? Are there tasks that could be performed in more efficient ways to focus on the true lawyering activities and shift to other labor or automation the less lawyer-required actions?

And so on.

The first and foremost way to cope with burdening workloads is to understand the who, what, where, why, and how that lies buried underneath the hours being logged. AI tools can be handy for this kind of analysis. Once you have comprehensively analyzed the workload landscape, this opens the door to mitigating the overwork conundrum. An individual lawyer might not readily be able to see the bigger picture per se. Only once a collective set of data across a law practice is explored can you more likely discover patterns and seek to balance or shift the overloading challenge.

One key point here is that a one-person legal shop is probably not going to glean much from an AI-based analysis of their workload efforts. The emphasis for Machine Learning is to chomp through lots and lots of data, which is only likely to be available in a relatively larger-sized law practice that has multitudes of attorneys at work.

This type of caseload analysis has been undertaken in other legal contexts too. For example, in an article covering data-driven legal caseloads for judges, the authors indicate: "For the judiciary to manage caseloads effectively, dispose of court business without delay and deliver quality service to the public, adequate resources are essential. Meeting this challenge requires states to assess objectively the number of judges required to handle caseloads, as well as whether judicial resources are being allocated equitably and used prudently. State court systems are increasingly using the weighted caseload method of judicial workload assessment as a best practice" (as indicated by authors Matthew Kleiman, Cynthia Lee, and Brian Ostrom in "Workload Assessment: A Data-driven Management Tool for the Judicial Branch," The Council Of State Governments).

Another avenue for the use of AI by law practices consists of employing AI-infused LegalTech that can speed up lawyering efforts or offload some legalese tasks to automation. These AI-powered capabilities are gradually getting added to conventional LegalTech and will ultimately become essential part-and-parcel components (we're not quite there as yet).

Conclusion

Senior partners and those managing a law practice should be conscientiously exploring the workloads of their attorneys. The notion is to avert burnout when possible and create a work climate that is alluring and retains or attracts the best legal talent to be found. Law practices that take a blind eye to such matters are apt to find themselves shedding top talent and ironically kicking into even higher gear the workload problem at their firm.

Make sure to use AI as a means to comprehend the lawyering workload and aid those unduly overworked attorneys and save your law practice correspondingly. AI in this case is not a panacea, but nor should it be ignored or overlooked.

Note: *For supplemental materials depicting the aspects discussed in this chapter, refer to Appendix B, which contains various augmented diagrams, charts, and additional related facets of relevance.*

CHAPTER 11

AI & LAW:
DO LAWS COVER AI

Key briefing points about this article:

- There was a time that *AI For Good* was captivating worldwide attention
- A bubble was burst upon the realization that *AI For Bad* also is taking place
- Into this morass comes the question of whether existing laws handle AI sufficiently
- One camp says our laws don't, while the other extreme camp says our laws do
- Using an existence proof ostensibly highlights a vital in-between nature thereof

Introduction

I'm going to bring you into the secret fold of knowing about a particularly vexing and caustic finger-pointing argument that pervades the advent of AI and the law.

First, for clarification, there are two major ways to intertwine AI and the law.

The most commonly expressed aspect entails applying AI to the law. For example, there are AI-based tools that allow lawyers to examine a vast corpus of court cases and find legal precedents that seem most befitting to a new case being litigated. Another example consists of using AI Natural Language Processing (NLP) technology to do online inquiries of submitted documents as part of an e-Discovery process.

And so on.

The other means of intermixing AI and the law consists of using our laws to govern AI.

You see, some believe that AI is becoming unruly and getting legally out of hand (illegally so). We've seen numerous circumstances of AI-embedded systems that exhibit inherent racial or gender biases, such as the concerns discovered about advanced facial recognition technologies. This had led to a strident call to apply the law to AI, presumably reining in the misuse and abusive elements of modern-day AI systems.

Applying The Law To Govern AI Is The Matter At Hand

Let's unpack the latter conundrum regarding the law as applied to AI.

The legal dilemma or outright vexing consideration is whether existing laws are sufficiently able to cover AI. There are some legal pundits that decry the weaknesses, omissions, and loopholes that permeate our existing laws when it comes to the oversight of AI. This viewpoint postulates that we need to quickly change, rewrite, or craft anew a series of laws that will properly contain and stifle the *AI For Bad* that is increasingly coming to the forefront.

When everyone was agog over the *AI For Good* that kept initially being promulgated and touted, there was little or no voiced concern about whether the laws were up to par about AI. As the *AI For Bad* began to appear, a realization struck home that perhaps the laws could not handle the legal twists presumably arising via the advent of AI.

Into the void stepped those stakeholders insisting that our laws were outmoded and needed an urgent refresh to cope with the evildoings of AI.

On the other side of this coin, some vehemently asserted that our laws on the books are just fine, thank you very much, and can readily contend with the emergence of advanced AI systems. In this perspective, AI is nothing more than various computer-based algorithms, for which we've had to contend with such computerization since the inception of computing.

Until the day that AI turns the corner and shifts into sentience, our existent laws can serve us well to adjudicate matters underpinning the *AI For Bad* outrages (the argument says). If somehow someday AI garners a sentient capacity, sure, we might need to anoint AI with some form of legal personhood (involving legal changes, likely notable ones, amid our laws). But nobody can seriously state when today's AI will make that future transformation, nor do we know that it will ever happen at all.

Does this indeed all turn on an all-or-nothing twist?

In other words, one camp seems to proclaim that our laws are adequate and no new laws are needed (nor are existing laws requiring any adjustments). This camp suggests that existing laws either already fit the bill, or we can simply reinterpret the laws to fit the bill. Any such reinterpretation does not necessitate changing the existing wording and instead consists entirely of reflecting mindfully about the scope and meaning of the laws, extending those laws over and upon the non-sentient AI.

The other camp appears to be on the extreme opposite side of this contentious matter. We must have new laws or at least demonstrably adjust our existing laws to sufficiently cope with today's AI. They eschew the idea that we would attempt to shoehorn prevailing laws into covering AI. This is seen as a desperate attempt to avert doing the hard work of deriving laws that comport with our contemporary times.

Bite the bullet, get our laws aligned to deal with AI, and as an added bonus be anticipating the far future such that the laws will have a long runway of being usable and applicable to whatever current AI eventually morphs or is advanced into (say these flag-wavers).

Those that are somewhere in the middle of the two camps would point out that an existence proof can readily undercut the extremism involved.

Essentially, if even one instance of an existing (adverse) AI system could be shown as not legally bound by our laws, this would seemingly shut down the argument that our existing laws are up to the judicial task of keeping AI in check. Likewise, though on the polar opposite side, if even one instance of an existing AI system could be shown as falling within the purview of existing laws, it would imply that at least some of our laws are able to cover AI.

So, the pragmatic in-betweener can merely cite AI-based facial recognition and the legal woes therein as a two-for-one special that covers both of those extreme proofs of existence showstoppers. We disprove that all laws do <u>not</u> cover AI, and we simultaneously disprove that all laws <u>do</u> cover AI.

The gist is that some of our laws do cover AI, while some of our laws do not cover AI.

By taking such a vantage point, we then shift the discourse into one that examines which of our laws as written are well-prepared for AI versus those laws that are either inadequate or we simply have a gaping hole of sorely needed applicable laws.

Furthermore, we can ask which legal cases and precedents fit the particulars of AI and which do not?

There is also the difficulty of pinning down what is AI and therefore comes within the AI-related laws since the AI moniker is altogether vague and can be construed exceedingly widely or used in a purposefully cunningly narrow way.

Conclusion

Bickering over the question of whether AI, as we know of it today, is within or beyond our laws is perhaps a false dichotomy. Putting legal energy toward elucidating what makes some laws unable to cover AI is presumably a more powerful focus.

This would lend credence to those exhorting that we are already in the midst of letting the AI horse out of the legal barn and that we need to shore things up before we find ourselves in a legal frenzy after the fact.

Note: *For supplemental materials depicting the aspects discussed in this chapter, refer to Appendix B, which contains various augmented diagrams, charts, and additional related facets of relevance.*

CHAPTER 12

AI & LAW: TUBRO-ENCABULATOR

Key briefing points about this essay:

- The turbo-encabulator dates back to the 1940s (be wary)
- Every few years since then, the turbo-encabulator seems to resurface
- We can use the turbo-encabulator to consider the status of AI in the law
- This is especially relevant given the advent of AI and Machine Learning in the law
- Important lessons are worthy of consideration and reflection thereof

Introduction

There is an eye-catching sign that grabs your attention since it blares in large-sized lettering to come and learn about the *turbo-encabulator* (what's that, you wonder).

You are at a prestigious innovation in the law conference and perchance come upon a LegalTech vendor showcasing the latest in AI for the law, proclaiming that their newly conceived and fully devised turbo-encabulator has miraculously and definitively solved the problem of attaining full-on AI-based legal reasoning.

No more wondering whether we will ever achieve the vaunted robo-lawyer or robo-judge. With this amazing turbo-encabulator component, the computer-based capability of rendering lawyering advice is utterly on par with that of human attorneys.

I assume that such a bold proclamation would garner your rapt attention.

And so it should.

One of the most vexing questions facing the intertwining of AI and the law entails the seeming impossibility of replicating the human-powered legal prowess possessed by lawyers and infusing this legal beagle know-how into computers. To date, legal informatics researchers and affiliated tech vendors have only dabbled around the far edges of what attorneys do when performing their legally minded services.

The suggestion that the wholescale embodiment of lawyering is finally packed into a computer system is a resounding surprise and cause for worthwhile inspection. You would hopefully be tempted to find out how this AI-based trickery has been accomplished. What exactly does the turbo-encabulator do, such that it can do everything that an everyday barrister can do?

You opt to take a look at their brochure and see this pointed language:

"For a number of years now, work has been proceeding apace in order to bring perfection to the crudely conceived idea of infusing legal acumen into a computer via AI. Achieving this milestone has required the invention of inverse reactive current for use in unilateral phase detractors, and furthermore required the construction of a capability to automatically synchronize cardinal grammeters."

The wording of the pamphlet leaves you a bit perplexed, scratching your head as you ponder the description, though you acknowledge in your own mind that you are a lawyer versed in legal language and admittedly you are not a techie versed in the steeped arcane world of technological language. We might facetiously say that just as Scotty professed in the *Star Trek* series that he's *just* an engineer, by gosh you are *just* an attorney (and not an engineer).

In any case, you continue to read the description:

"The breakthrough instrument is the turbo-encabulator. Now basically the key new principle involved is that instead of the legal knowledge being generated by the relative motion of conductors and fluxes, it is produced by the modial interaction of magneto-reluctance and capacitive diractance. The earlier and unsuccessful approaches had a base plate of pre-famulated amulite surmounted by a malleable logarithmic casing in such a way that two spurving bearings were in a direct line with a panametric fan. The latter consisted simply of six hydrocoptic marzlevanes, so fitted to the ambifacient lunar waneshaft that legal acumen was effectively prevented."

Well, that does provide a boatload of in-depth added explication, yet it kind of goes over your head. You stridently assume that this is all sensible to someone versed in the technical underpinnings of AI in the law. The verbiage certainly seems quite impressive.

The brochure proffers this notable concluding assertion:

The turbo-encabulator has now reached a high level of development, and it's being successfully used in the operation of novertrunnions. Moreover, whenever a forescent skor motion is required, it may also be employed in conjunction with a drawn reciprocation dingle arm, to reduce sinusoidal repleneration. For those seeking professional legal advice and legal services, the turbo-encabulator now makes tapping into online legal knowledge entirely feasible, ready to be used for ensuring adjudicational justice all of the time on a 24x7 basis, and instantly accessible to all."

Wow, this is entirely breathtaking. The only other question that comes to your mind is the pricing or expected cost to use the turbo-encabulator.

On top of this, you might be worrying that your future as an attorney is now marked. The fact that AI turned the corner and can do what lawyers do is both exciting and potentially depressing.

Could this be real?

The inarguable answer is that it is not real.

There isn't any such device and nor have there been any earthshattering breakthroughs as yet in terms of crafting AI-based legal reasoning systems. The hard work of trying to design and build AI for that particular purpose continues to slog on. Small and solely incremental improvements are the norm. Nobody has whisked together a magic wand to suddenly leapfrog us forward in this venerated pursuit.

Exposing The Turbo-Encabulator For What It Is

What then is a turbo-encabulator?

In a manner of speaking, you've just been had.

For those of you that might be aware of this persistent running gag in the tech field, the revered and totally fictionalized "turbo-encabulator" is an old-time piece of technobabble that keeps on earning its keep. Originally coined in the 1940s as an insider's knee-slapping piece of babbling narrative, the description is also pretty much word-for-word as it has always been portrayed.

I sheepishly admit that I inserted the aspects about AI and the law into the otherwise generic depiction of the notably hilarious turbo-encabulator conveyance.

Why so?

Two key lessons come to mind.

First, be very wary of LegalTech vendors that use tons of AI-specific buzzwords when describing their latest wares. The odds are that it is a bundle of technobabble, packed together to give you the impression that they have broken new ground and achieved something remarkable. Maybe yes, maybe not.

Second, when you meet with your clients and bombard them with legalese, in some sense you are using the same turbo-encabulator language that inevitably and exasperatingly seems quite foreign to them. If that's what you are aiming for, continue with the legal lingo barrages. Otherwise, try to shift into everyday plainspoken language.

Conclusion

I've also done something else by telling you about the turbo-encabulator.

You are now a member of an exclusive club, namely people that know about and spread the *good word* about the enthralling and best thing since sliced bread turbo-encabulator.

I'd bet that few of your attorney colleagues know about it, thus, you can now chide them mercilessly.

.

Note: *For supplemental materials depicting the aspects discussed in this chapter, refer to Appendix B, which contains various augmented diagrams, charts, and additional related facets of relevance.*

CHAPTER 13

AI & LAW: ASSEMBLY LINE LAWYERING

Key briefing points about this article:

- Assembly lines are well-known as being key to efficient mass production
- Manufacturing extensively uses assembly lines, as do fast-food eateries
- Concerns have been raised about assembly line pitfalls in our justice system
- Some have floated the notion of assembly lines in law practices for legal endeavors
- AI in the law could very likely spur and enable such law practice transformations

Introduction

They say that oil and water do not mix.

Perhaps the same could be said about the field of law and the overarching concept of assembly lines.

There has been much hand wringing over the years about the dangers of an assembly line approach to justice. Indeed, legal research has focused on the downsides of our judicial system devolving into a cookie-cutter form of adjudication, often referred to unkindly as McJustice (a sardonic take on the facet that fast food eateries employ assembly-line techniques, which analogously is predicted to sordidly overtake our courts and undercut the principles of justice).

As notably stated in a legal research article published in the *St. Louis University Law Journal*: "We're seeing court systems that are run about like a fast-food restaurant. A fast-food restaurant may be a little better, because at least there are some choices and a menu there for the customers. But people are processed through court not understanding what's happening to them, with no investigation by the lawyer, no understanding of who they are, when they're sentenced. They're just processed through the system" (per the article by Mark Milton, "Why Fools Choose to Be Fools: A Look at What Compels Indigent Criminal Defendants to Choose Self-Representation," 2009)

Core concepts that initially introduced the advantages of assembly-line production have often been credited to the famous economist Adam Smith in his treatise of 1776 entitled *The Wealth Of Nations*.

You might recall from your history books that in the eighteenth century, Adam Smith sketched out an assembly line method for manufacturing pins. In brief, pins at the time were handcrafted and took about 18 distinct steps to produce. One worker working alone would require quite a bit of time to craft a single pin. Even if you added a bunch more separately toiling workers, their productivity was still limited by the fact that each worker was serially creating a pin.

Adam Smith proposed that each worker could be devoted to some particular portion of the 18-steps and work in a collective way to produce pins. The pin would make its way along a line of workers. Each worker would perform their own specialized or specific task for the pin manufacturing effort.

We can jump forward in time and admire the use of assembly lines by Henry Ford and the Ford Motor Company in the early 1900s that led to mass production of automobiles and spurred widespread adoption of assembly-line techniques within many industries (for historical accuracy, it is argued by historians that Fordism of assembly line usage ought to be credited to teams of participants at Ford and not to Henry Ford singularly, plus the team at Ford was inspired by and owes due credit to a Chicago slaughterhouse they had visited and which used an assembly line for the butchering process).

The assembly line notion is revered in some instances and repulsed in others.

Because workers are said to be reduced to robotic-like actions, the general belief is that assembly lines only apply to so-called blue-collar occupations. Also, the further assumption is that an assembly line is blindly operated to produce only standardized results. This is a proverbial and oft denigrated one size fits all mantra.

There are all kinds of criticism leveled at assembly lines, some of which are off base but nonetheless a commonly accepted misconception.

Per the earlier mention of McJustice, the implied contention is that an assembly line for the processing of court cases is bound to run at too fast a pace (is that necessarily true?). People seeking justice are essentially ramrodded as though they are a piece of metal that is making its way along an assembly line and aiming to be molded into a pin. Critics would vehemently exhort that we ought to not treat humans as though they were inanimate objects such as a lowly everyday metal pin.

Law Offices And The Assembly Line Whisperer

Shifting gears, there is a whole other legal venue into which the assembly line possibility is at times postulated as being applicable, namely that law practices can leverage "assembly lines" for the legal endeavors of servicing their clients.

Yes, the idea is that rather than assigning one lawyer to one client, it might be beneficial to treat a client as though they are flowing down an assembly line within the law practice and be ergo aided by various attorneys at each stage of the legal case processing.

This smacks many lawyers as insulting.

They would insist that practicing the law is a craftsman or craftswoman endeavor. Attorneys are professionals and not rote-like automata (some say that lawyers are gold-collared knowledge workers). Assembly line legal services would be bad for attorneys, it is said, and likewise bad for clients, it is said.

Speaking of automata, there is a suggestion that the advent of AI in the law could enable an assembly line form of legal practice. Human lawyers would be augmented by the use of AI-based legal reasoning.

You see, one of the difficulties about using an assembly line approach in the use case of knowledge workers such as attorneys is the potential loss of knowledge about a client during each of the handoff stages or steps. To overcome this knowledge gap, the presumption is that an AI-based legal reasoning system could keep tabs on the legal matter at hand. This AI would then aid each attorney in the stepwise process, thusly making the flow of a client and their legal case into a presumed seamless activity.

For larger-sized law offices, the upside of an assembly line (we certainly won't call it that) would be that the precious and costly labor of the attorneys could be better utilized. This could allow for the handling of more clients. Some argue this would also reduce dependency upon a particular lawyer for a particular client, freeing up resources and allowing for heightened legal specialization versus being legal generalists. Etc.

Conclusion

Though it might be a blasphemous proposal, there is a valid argument to be made that an AI-augmented "assembly line" for lawyers proffering legal services could be good for the lawyers and good for the clients. One thing for sure is that the catchphrase of an assembly line will have to be dropped else there is little chance that any self-respecting law firm would want to adopt such practices.

What about streamlined full-service get-the-job-done legal services?

Maybe that needs some added work and further processing down the line.

Note: *For supplemental materials depicting the aspects discussed in this chapter, refer to Appendix B, which contains various augmented diagrams, charts, and additional related facets of relevance.*

CHAPTER 14

AI & LAW: AI FORENSIC VULNERABILITIES

Key briefing points about this essay:

- Most lawyers will inevitably encounter digital photos or digital video in their legal cases
- Forensic specialists are often hired to inspect the digital imagery
- These inspections can also entail digital transformations, such as enlarging images
- AI and especially Machine Learning are often the workhorse doing the transforms
- Lawyers need to realize that there are legally open questions that can arise

Introduction

Consider the old proverb that evil often lurks deep in the shadows.

Perhaps a more modern take on this shrewd adage is that untoward legal problems lurk within the confines of AI-based Machine Learning algorithms that at times empower those inscrutable image processing programs used for forensics analysis.

Let's unpack that hefty dose of techno-jargon that underpins this legal beagle eye-opening declaration.

First, you either have already or will someday be faced with a legal situation involving digitally captured photographic or video evidence. This seems inevitable for certainly any criminal defense attorney and even reasonably possible for a civil attorney. Our world today is awash in cameras. The ease of taking a photo or capturing a snippet of video is readily done by your smartphone, or perhaps a doorbell that has a video monitor, and so on.

These are all digital photos and digital videos.

This is markedly different than the age-old method of capturing images on film. If you tell someone from today's latest generation that we used to take a canister of film to a store to get it developed, and that we had to wait oftentimes days or more to get the produced pictures, the laughter and disbelief will spin your head.

Anyway, along with having photos and videos that are digitally recorded comes the advent of being able to use digitally based image processing tools. You can use software to examine the recorded images. Of course, nowadays even the worn-out line that a picture has been "photoshopped" is almost past its expiration date.

Everyone readily knows that you can use software to play all sorts of tricks on any digital image, including photos and videos.

I'll share with you a twist that should hopefully get your legal antenna on high alert. Someone using a software package to examine and that in any manner whatsoever impacts the digital content is likely unaware of how the image processing "magic" takes place.

This includes many presumed forensics experts. By and large, forensic experts learn how to use various software tools to conduct forensic analyses of digital content. They know which commands to use and how to essentially operate the software. What they don't know is the true underneath-the-hood particulars of how the software actually works.

You see, as I mentioned earlier, evil can lurk in the shadows, for which an everyday forensic expert has no clue as to what the evils are, nor how to ferret out the evilness. The turn of events on this mysteriousness is partially due to the use of AI-based techniques and technologies for image processing, especially the application of so-called Machine Learning (also sometimes referred to as Deep Learning).

What To Scrutinize About Machine Learning In Forensics Work

You can think of Machine Learning as a type of computational pattern matching.

Machine Learning software is programmed to try and find patterns within some presented data. The easiest way to envision this would be to hark back to your statistics classes wherein you played with linear regression. You might have collected data about people's height and weight, fed the data into a regression package, and voila discovered a statistical relationship associated with height and weight.

In the use case of image processing, software using Machine Learning is typically based on having had prior data and images that were used to "train" the algorithms implemented in the tool. As you'll see in a moment, the training data is a crucial telltale clue, and yet any ordinary forensics specialist is blissfully unaware of what training data might have been used for the particular package at hand (and, probably doesn't know which of the myriad of Machine Learning algorithms is specifically programmed into the code).

Suppose you have a somewhat blurry digital image that maybe has a person's head obscured behind other objects shown in a photo. You want to find out whether that portion of the image reveals that your client was at the scene in question. Let's assume that the whole matter is indubitably going to be a crucial piece of evidence, significant to either pretrial activities or to be used potentially at trial.

Assume that a forensic specialist uses a bona fide and presumably tried-and-true image processing package to enlarge the portion of the digital photo that contains a person's head. Upon doing so, the image of the head is now digitally much larger in size and appears to have a much greater semblance of clarity, arising as a result of the digital imagery manipulations (occurring somewhat via the commands issued by the forensic specialist using the package).

The forensic specialist has just used a black box of sorts to invoke the digital enlargement and digital cleanup of the image. It could be that the underlying Machine Learning algorithm has spuriously generated an enlarged image that departs demonstrably from the original snippet. Perhaps prior training data used to establish the parameters of the Machine Learning algorithm were based on heads that are not of the same kind. And so on.

You might recall that there have been many reported qualms about facial recognition technology that has at times contained inherent bias of a racial or gender nature. This is partially due to the algorithms used, but likely more so due to the data that was the training set for the facial recognition software.

Several legally disconcerting gotchas are part-and-parcel with AI-based Machine Learning algorithms.

The chances are that someone using a different package for the image processing would get a substantially different result, which is probable since the other package has been trained on some other set of data (plus, might have a variant of the Machine Learning algorithm used in the other tool).

Furthermore, the forensic specialist is likely unable to sufficiently explain how the tool did the digital transformations. All that the specialist can seemingly attest is that they used this command or that command, but they really are woefully ignorant of how the software accomplished those commands.

Conclusion

The gist of this discussion is that you cannot necessarily accept and nor should you blindly accept that a digitally manipulated image or video is somehow fully accurate and apt, even when a forensic specialist confidently asserts that they are using a so-called standardized forensic image processing package.

The devil is in the details.

Note: *For supplemental materials depicting the aspects discussed in this chapter, refer to Appendix B, which contains various augmented diagrams, charts, and additional related facets of relevance.*

CHAPTER 15

AI & LAW: EXPLAINABLE AI MEANINGFULNESS

Key briefing points about this essay:

- AI continues to be rolled out in an ever-increasing number of avenues
- Often, the AI contains algorithmic decision making (ADM) rendering key decisions
- Regulators are rapidly seeking to ensure that the AI also provides ADM explanations
- This is known as XAI or explainable AI
- For XAI, the notion of legal meaningfulness is becoming a core characteristic

Introduction

Not all explanations are necessarily handy or insightful.

An explanation might have no particular meaning to you. Sure, the explanation is laid out for you, but trying to make heads or tails of it is confounding. In that sense, we can reasonably ask or expect that a proper explanation should at least be meaningful.

A meaningful explanation would seemingly be a solid step forward in ensuring that the explanation can be useful. But the general vibe or notion of meaningfulness can be difficult to pin down.

In other words, if someone or something provides you an explanation, could you ascertain whether the explanation so provided is characterized as being meaningful?

Maybe yes, maybe no. A key crux of the problem hinges on exactly how we ought to define meaningfulness. In addition, once an explanation has been rendered, the next hurdle entails trying to assess the essence of the explanation against the defined notion of meaningfulness.

Some would say that this is all quite uncertain and murky.

Why then care about it?

Because the advent of AI has revealed the serious matter of getting the AI to explain how any of the algorithmically derived "decisions" have been generated. This rising area of the AI field is known generally as XAI or explainable AI. Rather than simply and solely having the AI emit some concluding message or outcome, we might reasonably also desire to have the AI divulge how the answer was divined. This is especially expected whenever there is an "algorithmic decision making" (ADM) process taking place.

There is going to be quite a pronounced legal brouhaha concerning AI and the explainability sufficiency thereof.

People that use or are subject to AI decision rendering will inevitably start demanding that the proverbial black box be opened to reveal what is going on inside. Regulators are realizing that this rising tide is looming ahead as the adoption of AI continues at a frenetic pace.

Something seemingly as mundane or innocuous as getting an explanation is going to become and already is a hot and trending topic in AI and the law.

Let's unpack this.

Digging Into The Details Of Meaningful Explanations

Suppose you decide to apply online for a home loan. There are no human agents that discuss your loan request with you, and instead, the entirety of the loan request process takes place via the use of filling in online forms. After completing the forms, the AI loan decision-making system indicates whether you are granted a home loan.

One might assume that if you were granted the loan, you likely aren't especially craving for an explanation. Perhaps you don't want to look a gift horse in the mouth, as it were. On the other hand, if the AI system turned down your loan request, the odds are pretty high that you would want to know why.

You would seemingly demand to know what led to the loan being disapproved. Besides innate curiosity, you certainly would have other quite bona fide reasons for seeking to discover what led to the turndown decision. Is the algorithmically derived decision based on some bias such as on racial or gender lines? What factors were used? Can you potentially take action to improve your chances of getting a loan in the future? Etc.

Legal scholar and experienced attorney Eran Kahana proffers that one crucial element of meaningfulness would involve the notion of the explanation being considered *understandable* and likens this to consumer credit reports: "The 'easily understood' quality is addressed with presenting the information in a familiar, proven format. The one I think that is suitable for the task is what we see in the consumer credit report. Credit reports are easily understood. They do not explain the precise correlation between a specific credit event and its precise impact on the FICO score. (Even if disclosed, it is likely difficult to understand.) All they inform the consumer about is that a certain, identified event caused their FICO score to increase or decrease by a number of points and that is why a certain financial decision was made; there is no explanation as to why only by x and not y points. Thus we can see that using XAI to identify the parameters (not methodology) used by the decision-making application and providing it in a way similar to a credit report would likely comply with the CPRA's "meaningful" requirement" (as indicated in "Using XAI To Comply With The California Privacy Rights Act," Stanford CodeX Blog, November 25, 2021).

When referring to the CRPA, this is the California Privacy Rights Act that was passed by California voters in November 2020 (known as Proposition 24) and both amended and simultaneously expanded the prior California Consumer Privacy Act (CCPA).

A portion of the CRPA ostensibly also covers the XAI topic, indirectly, via Section 1798.185(a) Subsection 16 that states this: "(16) Issuing regulations governing access and opt-out rights with respect to businesses' use of automated decision-making technology, including profiling and requiring businesses' response to access requests to include meaningful information about the logic involved in those decision-making processes, as well as a description of the likely outcome of the process with respect to the consumer."

As per the posting by Kahana, we might tie into this the draft set of *Four Principles Of Explainable Artificial Intelligence* that is available via the National Institute of Standards and Technology (NIST), known as NISTIR 8312, and which states this: "A system fulfills the Meaningful principle if the recipient understands the system's explanations. Generally, this principle is fulfilled if a user can understand the explanation, and/or it is useful to complete a task. This principle does not imply that the explanation is one size fits all." Of course, there is a lot more to meaningfulness, and the NIST study notes this quandary: "Therefore, meaningfulness is influenced by a combination of the AI system's explanation and a person's prior knowledge, experiences, and mental processes."

The legal obligation to provide AI explanations is argued as also already being required in the GDPR (General Data Protection Regulation, an EU regulatory set of laws that entail data protection and privacy aspects).

Several court cases have arisen in the EU that contended there was an apparent XAI requirement per Article 13 Section 2f: "(2f) the existence of automated decision-making, including profiling, referred to in Article 22(1) and (4) and, at least in those cases, meaningful information about the logic involved, as well as the significance and the envisaged consequences of such processing for the data subject."

Notice once again the use of the word "meaningful" as a recurring theme in the XAI matter (as stated in the GDPR's use of the phrase "meaningful information about the logic involved").

To clarify, the construct of being legally meaningful is only one prong of the many tests needed to establish that an XAI-produced explanation is worthwhile, apt, accurate, and substantive. You could presumably have a completely fabricated explanation that is patently false or sordidly misleading, and yet it could still appear to pass a *meaningfulness* requirement in a strict sense.

Conclusion

For those of you who are legal beagles wanting to join the AI in the law realm, roll up your sleeves and pitch in to figure out the legal underpinnings for XAI. One way or another, the odds are that this will all end up in the courts, and for many years to come, there will be bitter legal battles over whether AI systems are doing their duty when it comes to being explanatory.

I trust this suitably explains the need for meaningful explanatory AI.

Note: *For supplemental materials depicting the aspects discussed in this chapter, refer to Appendix B, which contains various augmented diagrams, charts, and additional related facets of relevance.*

CHAPTER 16

AI & LAW: LEGAL SUGAR

Key briefing points about this essay:

- Software engineers are familiar with the likes of so-called syntactic sugar
- This consists of embellishing program code for hopefully added clarity
- The semantics remain unchanged, just the syntax has been altered in cosmetic ways
- Perhaps our laws could benefit from having some syntactic sugaring take place
- AI for this purpose can be devised, though will struggle with averting semantic pitfalls

Introduction

Did you add some sugar to your food today?

I dare say that you did, whether you realize it or not (the sugar was likely already included). That being said, a wide variety of health-related concerns have admonished us to be careful about overdoing the rush toward sugaring our food. There is presumably a just right amount of sugar that our daily diets ought to include.

The word "sugar" has lots of meanings. Besides actual sugar that we drench our desserts with, there is the notion of someone emoting discourse that has a sugary flavor to it. An old adage is that you ought to include a grain of sugar in whatever you say to others, and meanwhile be on the watch for a grain of salt in anything others say to you.

Another variant of the sugaring notion is a well-known catchphrase within the field of software engineering stated as *syntactic sugar*. Specifically, the efforts to write computer programs or do coding can be undertaken by making use of so-called syntactic sugar, whereby you write lines of code that are embellished with flavorful annotations and stylistic adornment. This is considered an optional way to write your code.

There are many within the computer field that cherishes syntactic sugar. Be forewarned that there is an equally vocal segment that utterly eschews syntactic sugar.

The simplest way to think of syntactic sugar is that the code being written is embellished with facets that hopefully make the program easier to read and understand. By adding the sugaring elements, a developer will presumably convey what the code is doing, more so than if the sugar wasn't utilized. This allows other programmers to look at the code and glean what is going on.

In brief, by using syntactic sugar, the code will be hopefully more expressive.

Besides serving as an aid for other programmers that aren't already familiar with the code, the sugar is handy for the originating programmer. You see, a programmer might set aside their code for days or weeks at a time, and upon returning to the code, could be confused about what they had in mind at the time of writing the code. In theory, the sugar will prompt them to readily remember what the code is intended to achieve.

Note that an important criterion for syntactic sugar is that it is not required per se. If a coder decides to not use any sugar at all, the code is still the same as though the sugar was indeed added. The sugar is considered "syntactic" rather than semantic. This means that the code will do the same things when performed or executed by a computer, regardless of how much sugar there might be piled into the code.

Something that makes a *semantic*-oriented alteration to code would imply that the code will do different functions or actions in comparison to the absence or omission of those semantic coatings. Thus, in contrast, the inclusion of syntactic sugar is supposed to not alter in any manner whatsoever the functional aspects of the program.

The Long And Winding Sugary Road

A tremendous amount of debate ensues about whether certain kinds of syntactic sugar are worthy of use or whether they might inadvertently be worse than having avoided deploying the sugar at all.

An extremely simple example that is often used to illustrate this conundrum consists of the rudimentary operation involving adding a value of 1 to a given variable. The usual programming code might indicate that the variable N is to be increased by a count of 1, such as N = N + 1. Anyone with any algebra under their belt would certainly recognize this notation right away.

A syntactic sugary version might indicate this as the equivalent of stating N++.

The sugared version showcases two plus signs to indicate that the variable N is to be incremented by a count of 1.

Is this easier to understand than the former version of N = N + 1?

Some insist that it is easier (once you've memorized that the double plus signs mean to do an increment of 1). Furthermore, the expression of N++ averts the potential error of someone that might have written the original code as N = M + 1, wherein they accidentally referred to the variable M and had meant to refer to the variable N instead.

Anyway, others would claim that the N = N + 1 ought to be the sugary version and that the N++ is the non-sugared version. You can see how dizzying this can become. In whatever manner we define syntactic sugar, another crucial aspect is that we need to also have a defined means to desugar something. Code that is sugared should be able to be desugared.

Shifting gears, perhaps we can apply the sugaring notion to the field of law and the practice of law. As you likely know, there is a great deal of brouhaha that our laws are presumably a form of code, akin to code that exists when doing computer programming. If that is indeed the case, we might equally assert that law can be sugared, and that law can also be desugared.

We could do the sugaring by hand, or possibly use AI to aid or undertake the syntactic sugaring for us. An AI system would take as input an existent set of laws and produce as output the syntactic sugar equivalent. On the other side of that coin, we might also have an AI system that can receive as input a set of laws that contain syntactic sugar, which the AI then outputs a desugared set of laws.

The rationale for sugaring our laws would be that the laws as they usually are written tend to be arcane and difficult to comprehend. A conversion via an AI-based legal syntactic sugaring system would aim to produce the same set of laws but made in a more readable fashion. People would no longer be perplexed by the laws.

Sounds great.

There are plenty of problems though with applying syntactic sugar to legal text. Recall that a key cornerstone is that the syntax changes are not to impact the semantics. The odds are that in everyday natural language, unlike the constrained nature of programming languages, even the smallest of syntactical changes will open Pandora's box of semantic interpretation changes.

Lawyers are likely to find cunning ways to contend that a law expressed in a syntactically altered way no longer has the identical semantic meaning as it once did. As such, we effectively would end up with two sets of laws that are not at all the same, and get embroiled in legal arguments about which prevails.

Conclusion

The serious question arises as to whether any amount of syntactic sugar in the law is too much sugar.

Maybe syntactic sugar for the law is a sweet idea, but even just a pinch of it could wreak legally sweetened havoc.

Note: *For supplemental materials depicting the aspects discussed in this chapter, refer to Appendix B, which contains various augmented diagrams, charts, and additional related facets of relevance.*

CHAPTER 17

AI & LAW: LEGAL LATIN KEYSTONES

Key briefing points about this essay:

- Lawyers are usually well versed in the cornerstone precepts of today's rule of law
- These are now famous legal precepts that stem from earlier Latin terminology
- For example, we accept at face value that there shall be no penalty without law
- In the push toward using AI to embody the law, we need to keep such precepts in mind
- AI must be devised such that ensures these bedrock principles remain intact and active

Introduction

Lawyers are taught a baseline of value statements that serve as linchpins for the rule of law (as we know of if it today). Usually couched in Latin terminology, these are sayings that have pretty much stood the test of time.

One such keystone is this: *Nulla poena sine lege.*

You might recognize that famous Latin catchphrase from your law school days. This bedrock legal principle states that there shall be no penalty without law. The essence of this revered precept assures that you can only be held accountable to the law when there is in fact some law that prohibits a behavior that ostensibly might be considered unlawful.

There is nothing axiomatic about such a proclamation.

Mankind has always held out the possibility that you can readily be punished or held accountable for breaking a law even if no such law exists or has ever existed. That's just the way the cookie crumbles, as they say. Gradually, humanity somewhat realized the inherent unfairness of not abiding by such a rule. You can say that we now generally seem to hold dear as a widespread value judgment that the "no penalty without law" belief ought to be a solid foundation for society and esteemed integrity for the rule of law.

What about AI that is used to embody our laws and serve them up on a legal platter to us?

In short, if we proceed apace to apply AI to the law, it seems sensible to ask whether or not the pinnacle precept of *nulla poena sine lege* will still apply. The obvious answer would be that of course, we would expect AI to abide by the solemn pledge of no penalty without law. Any consideration otherwise is beyond the pale.

The Legally Embedded Enigma And AI

The reason that I bring up this particular rule of law principle is that we do not know for sure that the venerated notion would in fact be held true via AI. Some legal researchers wring their hands about the possibility that we would paint humanity into a rather untoward corner by eventually extensively applying AI to the law.

Allow a moment to elaborate on this.

Suppose we start feeding the law into AI systems. This provides a variety of handy advantages. Rather than consulting the raw and inactive text of laws, we could use a computer system capability leveraging AI-based computational legal reasoning. The AI would interpret and elucidate the law. In that sense, the law becomes enlivened as though it has a form of agency underlying it.

Before we go off the rails about this, we should first all agree that this does not take us into the murky and highly speculative realm of sentience. The AI being depicted does not necessarily need to have sentience. A sentient form of AI is a whole different ballgame. As an important side note, we do not yet have any semblance of sentient AI, plus there is absolutely no viable indication that we are on the path toward such AI.

I'm not saying never and only cautioning care in making any leap of faith in that regard.

Returning to the Latin coined legal principle of no penalty without law, a qualm about using AI in the aforementioned role of seemingly embodying our laws and relating our laws back to us is that the AI might cross a bridge too far, as it were.

The non-sentient AI could computationally get ahead of itself. When the AI is inquired as to whether a particular act by someone has transgressed the laws, the AI might respond that indeed the act described is unlawful. The AI proffering this declaration might though miss the mark on the *no penalty without law* proviso.

It could be that the AI has been programmed in a manner that the computational processing infers that the act is unlawful, yet no specific law is associated with the unlawful stated assertion. Depending upon whether we accept a ruling from an AI-based black box that provides no means of explaining the legal decisions being rendered, we could have just stepped beyond the bounds of *nulla poena sine lege*.

An obvious way out of this conundrum would be to require that the AI emit an explanation, a capability generally known as XAI or explainable AI. Upon seeing the legally claimed elucidation by the AI, we could then judge whether the AI has stayed within bounds or gone outside them.

A caveat is that if we have become so reliant on AI for lawyering tasks that we no longer have human lawyers available, presumably the explanation might do us little good and we would scratch our heads as to whether the explanation provides proper legal grounding or not. Another qualm would be that the explanation is somehow utterly incomprehensible. Yet another concern is that the AI is unable to generate a bona fide and applicable explanation, or generates a seemingly plausible and yet entirely false explanation. Etc.

All of this just touches the surface on the relevant akin legal principles.

Let's add this one: *Nulla poena sine lege praevia*

You might recognize that notable Latin saying as the legal belief that we should avoid retroactive application of laws or otherwise keep away from ex post facto criminal laws. As an indication of how this could arise in an AI context, suppose upon being presented with an alleged act, the AI generates a "new" law that is suggested as being applicable to the act in question, despite the true facet that the AI did not have such a law on the books prior to the current moment of deriving said law.

That is a legally backdating kind of dilemma.

We can toss a bunch of other prominent precepts into this legally charged AI bucket. We have *nulla poena sine lege scripta* that suggests that there be no penalty without written law, and that a close cousin is the *nulla poena sine lege certa* or that law needs to be well-defined. An AI system containing our laws and for which is the sole diviner of our laws could easily deviate or violate those legal cornerstones.

Conclusion

Do not take this as a form of anti-AI diatribe. The potential for using AI in the law is tremendous and we should stridently continue toward attaining full-on AI-based legal reasoning.

The overarching point is that we should not lose our heads in that lofty pursuit, and we need to keep in mind and program solidly into the AI a prudent, reliable, and provable method of ensuring that these venerated mankind-devised legal precepts are retained and observed at all times.

.

Note: *For supplemental materials depicting the aspects discussed in this chapter, refer to Appendix B, which contains various augmented diagrams, charts, and additional related facets of relevance.*

CHAPTER 18

AI & LAW:
AI JURY SIMULATIONS

Key briefing points about this essay:

- Juries and juror behavior is vital factor for lawyers and lawyering
- Jury research has been ongoing since the earliest days of jury trials
- A prevailing approach has been the use of mock jurors in simulated trials
- Advances in computing have led to remote online mock jury research efforts
- AI is taking the mock jury to a new level and will transform jury research

Introduction

Lawyers care a lot about juries.

Any attorney undertaking a jury trial is bound to be grappling with a litany of concerns about the prospective jurors and the final chosen set of jurors.

Which jurors would seem best suited for the legal case at hand and are amenable or likely to be persuaded by the arguments that will be proffered by your side of the case? During a trial, the odds are that you are scrutinizing their every move and facial expression. Etc.

There is an abundance of research about juries.

Law schools usually cover some of the insights gleaned from the plethora of jury research findings. In addition, the odds are that budding lawyers will be inundated with seat-of-the-pants advice from seasoned attorneys about what supposedly works or doesn't work when it comes to trying cases and coping with juries.

When considering the behaviors of juries, you can divide the matter into two intertwining elements.

First, there is the particular behavior of individual jurors. This focus entails getting into the mind of jurors and anticipating how they might react or respond during legal proceedings. The assumption is that jurors can be distinctly typified based on identifiable characteristics, such as their disclosed background or perhaps by their courtroom demeanor while seated in the jury box.

The second key element, which is often neglected or simply overlooked, involves how jurors act or react when conferring in a group setting, namely while deliberating with their fellow jurors. You see, it is one thing to try and gauge a juror when they are observing and digesting a legal case, while it is something potentially altogether different to predict their group-oriented behavior that will emerge during the jury deliberations.

One of the most famous movies about the trial experience is the 1957 now-classic *12 Angry Men* film and its depiction of what presumably can occur once a jury engages in their deliberations. For those of you that haven't yet seen the venerated movie, it is a fascinating lesson in what can occur when the group dynamics get underway in a jury room. The movie begins with the jury getting final instructions from the judge and then trudging into the jury room.

We do not know what the jurors might have done during the trial itself and instead only see a fly-on-the-wall perspective as they come together and carry out their jury deliberations.

Anyway, the key point is that looking solely at individual jurors is not sufficient and we need to also calculate how the jury as a whole will interact and deliberate.

This salient notion of incorporating individual and group dynamics is what makes doing jury research an arduous endeavor. Legal researchers can usually easily get access to and examine mock jurors on an individual basis. All you need to do is put out an announcement of seeking experimental subjects, possibly provide some reward or honorarium for participating, and if looking at individual behavior you can administer written or oral tests of one kind or another.

Much tougher to pull off is putting together mock jurors as though they are collectively in a mock jury altogether. You need to coordinate their schedules. You have to ensure that they all are willingly able to act in their juror roles, which can sometimes break down when they find themselves in the presence of others. Many other qualms arise, such as if they are tossed together for a half-hour of mock jury deliberations, this could be said to be a far cry from real trials whereby the jurors have sat next to each other for perhaps days at a time and gotten to somewhat know each other informally.

A handy assessment of jury research methods is described by legal scholars Brian Bornstein and Amy Kleynhans in a *Denver Law Review* article entitled "The Evolution Of Jury Research Methods: From Hugo Munsterberg To The Modern Age" (2019), and keenly indicate the tradeoffs entailing various experimental approaches that have been undertaken in this realm. Mock jurors and mock juries can be examined in numerous ways, including but not limited to the use of direct observation, interviewing, archival analysis of jury verdicts, field studies, by the use of simulations, and so on.

Mock Jury Simulations Plus AI

In modern times, the use of simulations has become the preferred method overall, as per the article: "Simulations are currently the predominant method for studying both jurors and juries, and they are well-suited for studying both processes and outcomes." The usual approach to a simulation consists of bringing together a set of mock jurors, they are in some fashion brought up to speed about a fictional legal case (possibly based on prior cases or anticipated future cases), and then engaged as a jury to deliberate. Throughout the simulation, the experimenters are typically observing and taking notes of what the jurors are doing, and then at the conclusion of the simulation, there is post-analysis done that might involve interviewing the jurors either individually or as a group.

These efforts are usually augmented via the use of computers, such that the mock trial and the mock jury deliberations occur online and might involve a computer simulation guiding them. These are known as computer-mediated mock jury experiments.

The latest twist adds AI into the picture.

Per the researchers: "One modification to the computer-mediated deliberation paradigm, as described above, would be to incorporate it with artificially intelligent software." Furthermore, as an example of how this might arise, they mention this kind of augmentation: "A more sophisticated program, drawing on artificial intelligence could produce more nuanced responses by the confederates, which would provide greater realism (thereby reducing suspicion) while also generating a richer dataset."

On an overarching basis, these four major AI-related facets categorize mock jury efforts:

1) Mock jury with humans only and physically in-person
2) Mock jury with humans only that are interacting online and remotely
3) Mock jury with humans that interact directly with AI-based robo-jurors
4) Mock jury consisting entirely and solely of AI-based robo-jurors

In the instance of a mock jury of human mock jurors that interact with AI-based mock robo-jurors, there are two primary variants. If the AI robo-juror functionality is good enough, the mock jury human deliberators are not told that their "fellow jurors" include AI (this is a kind of Turing Test of sorts). When the AI is not up to par for that kind of pretense, the human jurors are informed that the mock effort encompasses AI systems.

The fourth category that consists of using solely AI-based mock robo-jurors is still being worked out. Though this can be done in extremely simplistic ways today, it is not anywhere close to providing much insight since the AI robo-jurors are demonstrably unlike human mock jurors.

Conclusion

Advancements in AI will presumably proffer greater capabilities and inevitably allow for human attorneys to hone their legal beagle skills via carrying on mock trials with a set of twelve AI-based robo-jurors that are able to simulate the behaviors of human jurors.

Some bemoan this possibility, wringing their hands that it might be a slippery slope toward our society shifting existent real-world trials into using AI-based robo-jurors, absent of any human jurors. This would undoubtedly raise all kinds of legal issues as to having our sacrosanct belief of a trial by one's peers being potentially upended.

.

Note: *For supplemental materials depicting the aspects discussed in this chapter, refer to Appendix B, which contains various augmented diagrams, charts, and additional related facets of relevance.*

CHAPTER 19

AI & LAW:

AI AS THIRTEENTH JUROR

Key briefing points about this essay:

- There is no doubt that a jury trial is one of the cornerstones of our form of adjudication
- Twelve jurors are the usual standard, all of whom are expected to act impartially
- A popular catchphrase involves referring to a thirteenth juror
- Besides a metaphorical reference, some argue that we do in fact need to add a juror
- Though the assumption is that the 13th juror is a human, perhaps AI will suffice instead

Introduction

You might have noticed that there are plenty of stories, stage plays, movies, and headlines that from time to time tout the notion of a thirteenth juror.

This of course is a twist on the aspect that juries are typically composed of twelve jurors in various adjudication contexts.

By referring to a thirteenth juror, the implication is that there are ways in which a jury might be considered augmented or expanded, which can be construed as a good thing or instead as a terrible possibility, depending upon your viewpoint on the matter.

One use of a thirteenth juror notion is the situation entailing a judge that opts to overtake a jury verdict.

We generally accept the practice that a judge might believe that the jurors were unreasonable in their deliberative result. Though the judge is presumably supposed to normally serve solely as a kind of umpire during a trial, there is a provision at times that the trial judge can declare on an "independent" basis that the jury insufficiently weighed the evidence and ergo arrived at an unjust decision.

The reason this is presumed as an "independent" rendering by the trial judge is that the judge did not partake in the jury deliberations per se and therefore was not an actual member of the jury. Instead, the judge was a de facto and distinctly separate "13th juror" for that trial.

There are plenty of other variants about a thirteenth juror.

Some legal researchers have argued that other outside factors could be labeled as a metaphorical thirteenth juror. For example, an article by Mark Geragos in the *Loyola Of Law Angeles Law Review* entitled "The Thirteenth Juror: Media Coverage Of Supersized Trials" (2006) proffers the assertion that the media coverage of a trial could be interpreted as a kind of thirteenth juror in some instances. This means that the reporting and social media surrounding a trial can act as powerfully as though a conventional jury of twelve had added the media as an additional juror: "In one such case I was involved with, the appellate court reversed a conviction because evidence made its way into the jury room that was never presented in the courtroom but was pervasively discussed in the media" (so indicates Geragos).

Moving beyond a metaphorical thirteenth juror, there is an occasional outstretched floated idea of actively increasing the number of jurors from twelve to in fact thirteen as a new kind of standard.

It seems that few are enamored of this somewhat unorthodox proposition (i.e., little if any bona fide legal justification seems to be put forth for a thirteenth *ordinary* juror position).

We can add a bit of twist though to the thirteenth juror role and ostensibly arrive at a more compelling rationale for including an additional juror.

Before we get to the drumroll reveal of that teaser, let's review what a juror is supposed to be. As foundationally indicated by Chief Justice John Marshall in the U.S. Supreme Court case of the *United States v. Burr,* 25 F. Cas. 49, 50 (C.D.D. Va. 1807): "The great value of the trial by jury certainly consists in its fairness and impartiality. Those who most prize the institution, prize it because it furnishes a tribunal which may be expected to be uninfluenced by an undue bias of the mind."

The crux here is that we prefer that our jurors do not have any special capability as a juror and otherwise purposely seek out those that essentially are oblivious as to the triers of facts role. Per legal researcher William Schwarz: "The jury trial, at best, is the apotheosis of the amateur. Why should anyone think that twelve persons brought in from the street, selected in various ways, for their lack of general ability, should have any special capacity for deciding controversies between persons" (in the Foreword to the book *The Jury: Tools of Kings* by Lloyd Moore, 1973).

This then brings us to the perhaps more convincing reason to have a thirteenth juror. Some argue that the thirteenth juror would be a "professional juror" that is versed in the matters of juries and the judicial processes of trials and adjudication. The other twelve jurors would have at immediate hand an especially trained and presumably certified "juror professional" that could aid the jury during its deliberations. Rather than each jury always having to reinvent the wheel as to how to carry out jury deliberations, an expert at such matters is seamlessly among them.

Finding The Best Possible Thirteenth Juror

Seems sensible on the surface.

I'm sure though you are instantly exhorting a plethora of reasons that this is an assuredly bad idea. Would this added juror have an equal vote? Would this thirteenth juror unduly sway the other jurors? Suppose the thirteenth juror carried their own personal opinions and preferences into the jury box, which then subtlety and silently biases the rest of the jury? Etc.

A twist on the twist of the thirteenth juror is to make the added and presumed human juror into instead being an AI-based robo-juror, as it were. Trials entailing twelve jurors would have an added "juror" that consists of an AI system tailored for the particulars of juries and jury deliberations (this could be the case for other sized juries too).

The logic underpinning using an AI-based "juror" is that the AI would potentially avert the qualms about the biases introduced by using an added human juror. In theory, the AI would act without any bias or preference as to the outcome of the trial (note: please be wary of such an AI purity claim).

The AI would be provided to guide the jurors in the process of their deliberations. This assistance would be bounded accordingly.

A further step would be that the AI could keep tabs on the jurors, essentially monitoring the jury deliberations. This would be a means of catching jurors that might be going outside their permitted legal functionality or that exhibit behavior tantamount to a form of juror misconduct. Whether this is a suitable use of such AI is an open question and some lament that the AI could be a chilling oppressive influencer of otherwise fair and impartial jurors.

Conclusion

Should AI be added to juries and become a thirteenth juror, either in a literal sense or perhaps primarily in a virtual loosey-goosey sense?

The framers of our Constitution and particularly per the essence of the 6th Amendment would have not likely envisioned the possibility of automation serving in this capacity. If AI can materially contribute to the ideals of an impartial jury, perhaps the radically unthinkable thirteenth juror as AI deserves a modicum of attention.

Time to float a trial balloon and test the waters.

Note: *For supplemental materials depicting the aspects discussed in this chapter, refer to Appendix B, which contains various augmented diagrams, charts, and additional related facets of relevance.*

CHAPTER 20

AI & LAW: JURY CONTAMINATION AND MISCONDUCT

Key briefing points about this essay:

- We can likely all agree that a core precept of our laws is the right to a trial by jury
- Not just any jury will do per se, since we also require a fair and impartial jury
- Pretrial contamination can adversely affect the fair and impartial aspiration
- During the trial, there can be further contamination, along with juror misconduct
- Various methods are used to detect these juror transgressions, including now AI

Introduction

Trial by jury is simultaneously a seemingly simple concept and yet also heralds one of the most important principles underlying our Constitutional rights and the bond we have between us the people, our government, and our laws.

As foundationally indicated by Chief Justice John Marshall in the U.S. Supreme Court case of the *United States v. Burr,* 25 F. Cas. 49, 50 (C.D.D. Va. 1807): "The great value of the trial by jury certainly consists in its fairness and impartiality. Those who most prize the institution, prize it because it furnishes a tribunal which may be expected to be uninfluenced by an undue bias of the mind."

The thing is, there are lots of ways that the fairness and impartiality of a jury trial can be readily undermined. In short, it is a lofty and crucial precept to want a jury to imbue fairness and impartiality, but reality can quickly undercut that outsized desired attainment.

Let's first consider the human foibles that can distort the role of serving as a juror.

Some prospective jurors are prone to faking what their true intentions are (versus someone simply seeking to genuinely serve as a fair and impartial juror). These so-called "stealth jurors" have a plethora of hidden and insidious reasons for pursuing the calling of being a juror. This is especially pronounced for those media-frenzied legal cases that have captured widespread public attention.

These sneaky prospective jurors might be hoping to strike publicity gold via serving on such a jury. They intend to garner their fifteen minutes of global fame due to being a juror on a notably media-boosting court case. Besides a wishful celebrity status, they are likely banking on a hefty book deal or maybe even a movie star role arising from their juror-tells-all saga.

Of course, there is a variety of other juror-related adverse predilections involved too.

A juror might claim they are impartial and yet be desperately striving to get onto a court case so that they can ensure a conviction if at all feasible. Likewise, a potential juror asserting that they are completely open-minded might be harboring a fervent desire to acquit, regardless of what the evidence shows.

Added on top of all these juror facades are the demonstrative impacts from pretrial contamination.

Given the ubiquitous nature of mass media and social media, the idealistic notion that jurors can be found that have not been tainted by pretrial online opinions and fakery is gradually wearing thin. Of course, there are assorted remedies that purportedly can cope with pretrial contamination: "The techniques used to minimize the impact of bias include using the voir dire process to exclude biased jurors, moving the trial to a venue not so permeated with publicity, granting a continuance until the publicity dies down, imposing a gag order on trial participants, sequestering the jury to reduce their exposure to publicity, and admonishing the jury to ignore publicity surrounding the trial" (as stated by Mark Geragos, in "The Thirteenth Juror: Media Coverage Of Supersized Trials," *Loyola of Los Angeles Law Review*, 2006).

It seems that such remedies are potentially on their last legs, per the dour further indication by legal researcher Geragos: "However, these remedies have proven to be demonstrably ineffective when there is a high level of prejudice against the defendant. Even the two most commonly used techniques, voir dire and change of venue, have ceased to adequately guarantee that a fair and impartial jury will be impaneled."

Notably, there is more than just the pretrial shenanigans to be dealt with.

During a trial, the potential for jury contamination remains always within reach. This can occur in a somewhat juror unawares fashion, but it can also take place via the overt overreach and outright misconduct of jurors.

People are so accustomed to using social media that they are likely to do so while serving as a juror, even despite any stern and clear-cut warnings that a trial judge has conveyed as part of overarching jury instructions.

In an article published by the *Duke Law & Technology Review*, legal researchers Amy St. Eve and Michael Zuckerman describe instances of jurors that sent out tweets during jury deliberations, used Facebook to make postings about jury discussions, and otherwise seemed to impulsively and uncontrollably use social media (as examined in "Ensuring An Impartial Jury In The Age Of Social Media," 2012).

Some of this misconduct was said to be unintended and only spurred by habit, while in other instances the juror was acting in a stealth capacity to grab the brass ring and get their perniciously sought fame or fortune. No matter what the claimed basis for these acts, these *transgressions* still undercut the perceived and at times actual semblance of a fair and impartial jury.

Transgressions Aplenty Need Powerful Means To Stop Them

One newer legal beagle armament to fight against these transgressions involves the use of AI.

AI can help to rein in these juror contaminants and curb the likewise woeful misconduct activities. AI is gradually becoming part and parcel of the legal field, providing advanced computing to support and enhance the practice of law and the efforts of judicial endeavors.

Consider AI as being used to detect and warn when jurors are veering off the path of fairness and impartiality.

This AI is devised and utilized in two major venues:

1) AI systems for inside the courtroom juror-transgressions
2) AI systems for outside the courtroom juror-transgressions

First, AI can be used to try and catch jurors that transgress while inside the courtroom or courthouse.

For example, a prospective juror that opts to post to social media while in the midst of a juror queue for voir dire can be potentially spotted online via an AI-based searching tool that is programmed to examine vast swaths of emerging postings. This same AI can be used once the jurors are selected and serving on a seated jury. And, used upon the jury entering into their case deliberations.

Second, AI that emphasizes outside the courtroom transgressions can be notably useful during the pretrial stage. The AI searches for social media postings and other online aspects that might indicate the true nature of the prospective jurors and suss out the stealth jurors especially so.

Conclusion

There are though caveats to be considered.

Some worry that all this AI investigatory automation will cause prospective jurors to back out of serving on juries. Bona fide jurors that believe themselves to be fully fair and impartial could get the chills at having a Big Brother surveilling capacity watching their every online move. In brief, the effort to catch and cull the bad overstepping jurors could dry up the pool of sincere ones.

It is politely said that AI used in the juror transgression pursuit will have to be reined in to ensure that it does not assume that all jurors are guilty until proven innocent (as it relates to serving fairly and impartially).

Note: *For supplemental materials depicting the aspects discussed in this chapter, refer to Appendix B, which contains various augmented diagrams, charts, and additional related facets of relevance.*

CHAPTER 21

AI & LAW: JUROR IMPARTIALITY

Key briefing points about this essay:

- Trial by jury is a cornerstone of our judicial beliefs and adjudication ecosystem
- Jurors are required to be and remain impartial throughout a trial
- Sometimes a juror takes overt acts that reveal they are not impartial
- Other times a juror might subtly shift beyond impartiality
- A vexing question is whether the use of AI in the courtroom could spur juror partiality

Introduction

There is a sacred belief and endeared trust in our precepts of justice as sown via the revered *trial by jury*.

As foundationally indicated by Chief Justice John Marshall in the U.S. Supreme Court case of the *United States v. Burr,* 25 F. Cas. 49, 50 (C.D.D. Va. 1807): "The great value of the trial by jury certainly consists in its fairness and impartiality. Those who most prize the institution, prize it because it furnishes a tribunal which may be expected to be uninfluenced by an undue bias of the mind."

A juror has to be impartial throughout the *entirety* of a trial. If at any point a juror seems to transgress and no longer is impartial, the due process might be violated and appropriate legal remedies might be required.

To try and ensure due process, a trial judge is supposed to be ever vigilant to watch for jurors that seemingly cross the red line of partiality: "Due process means a jury capable and willing to decide the case solely on the evidence before it, and a trial judge ever watchful to prevent prejudicial occurrences and to determine the effect of such occurrences when they happen" (U.S. Supreme Court, *Smith v. Phillips*, 455 U.S. 209, 1982).

In some instances, the mark of impartiality might be readily apparent and easy to spot. Suppose for example that a juror uses their smartphone during a trial to send out a social media tweet indicating that the defendant is a rogue and "obviously guilty" of the stated crimes. This can be digitally detected online and provides rather inarguable implications that the juror has obviated their pledge of impartiality.

The Subtle Shift From Impartiality And The AI Aura

Consider though the more subtle ways that juror impartiality can be compromised.

A recent court case in California entailed a vexing question about how juror mindsets can be potentially altered while a trial is underway (see the case 2021 DJDAR 11565, *The People v. Donte Latraille Revels*, California Court of Appeals). In brief, a medical doctor had earlier performed an autopsy and was called by the prosecution to testify as an expert witness in a murder case. After giving such testimony, a juror perchance and on an unrelated basis became unconscious in the jury box. The medical doctor rushed to aid the juror (minimal treatment was rendered).

At first glance, this perhaps seems not especially noteworthy in that the juror turned out to be okay and the medical doctor abided by an ethical duty to provide medical aid as per the Hippocratic oath. All in all, though this is a rare and footnote-worthy kind of act in a courtroom, we would seem hard-pressed to make any more heyday about the come-and-gone matter.

The defendant upon being found guilty had his attorney file for a mistrial. You can perhaps guess what the claimed basis consisted of. The argument made was that the jurors and certainly the particular juror that became ill were likely swayed by the valiant act of the medical doctor and therefore were biased favorably toward the testimony of the medical doctor. This would seem a wholly natural inclination on the part of the jurors. Whereas the doctor at first was just one of the numerous witnesses, the outreach and aid to the unconscious juror would have ostensibly raised the trustworthiness of the doctor in the eyes of the jury.

The point herein is that there doesn't necessarily need to be an explicit indication that a juror has veered beyond impartiality. The mere exposure or presence of something that could impact their impartiality might alone do the trick of undercutting their neutrality.

I don't want to further linger on the case involving the unconscious juror, but I expect that you are earnestly wondering how the mistrial attempt turned out. Well, as additional background, during the trial the judge individually polled the jurors to ask whether the medical aiding act of the doctor had impacted their impartiality. They each stated that they still were and could remain impartial.

At appeal, the appellate indication was that the judge had seemingly sufficiently apprised whether there was any prejudice on the part of jurors, of which none was indicated, and that a fair trial had ergo occurred.

Shifting gears, consider that AI is gradually going to be utilized by attorneys, judges, and the like as part of our judicial ecosystem. AI-based legal reasoning systems are anticipated to serve as an aid to lawyers and jurists. This will happen outside the courtroom during preparations for trials, and can also occur inside a courtroom by a judge accessing an AI system or attorneys doing so while a trial is underway.

Let's now connect the dots on the topic of AI in the law and the matter of juror impartiality.

Imagine that a court case is underway. The jurors are seated and watching closely the actions of the judge and the attorneys. Much of the time, the attorneys will bring their notes up with them when questioning witnesses. Those handwritten physical notes are inevitably giving way to the use of electronic notes that a lawyer keeps on their iPad or similar handheld digital device.

Suppose an attorney arguing a part of the case is being aided by an AI-based legal reasoning system that is running on their handheld device. The attorney slips casually into the dialogue that the AI system has identified an inconsistency in the testimony of a key witness.

Is this cause for a potential mistrial?

You might be puzzled why such an outsized contention should arise. The logic is that if the jurors have prior experience with AI systems, or even if they don't but have predetermined beliefs about AI, the mere mention of AI as taking part in the trial could impact juror impartiality. Some jurors might love AI and think it can do no wrong, whereas others might hate AI that for example turned them down for some desired home mortgage loan.

Conclusion

All told, the notion is that any known use of AI in the courtroom by the attorneys or the judge could shape or distort the mindset of the jurors, assuming of course that the jurors become aware that AI is being used. You might be tempted to say that this is hogwash, namely that trying to ascribe juror partiality or impartiality as a result of merely using an AI tool is an extraordinary and altogether preposterous proposition.

Maybe so, or maybe not.

You stridently need to anticipate that such legally novel claims are heading in the direction of a judicial ecosystem that will slowly (ever so slowly) and yet inexorably embrace AI capabilities.

Note: *For supplemental materials depicting the aspects discussed in this chapter, refer to Appendix B, which contains various augmented diagrams, charts, and additional related facets of relevance.*

CHAPTER 22

AI & LAW: CHEWBACCA DEFENSE

Key briefing points about this article:

- Lawyers have likely seen their fill of inane arguments that veer into being nonsensical
- A handy and popular catchphrase for such argumentation is the Chewbacca defense
- The naming is from a famous South Park episode that skewered the O.J. Simpson case
- Shifting gears, AI-based legal reasoning systems can aid the crafting of legal arguments
- A vexing question is whether the AI should offer any Chewbacca defense suggestions

Introduction

Let's discuss legal argumentation.

I'm sure that you must know the famous or indubitably infamous line that if the glove doesn't fit then you must acquit. You might also know that this same facet underlies the so-called Chewbacca defense. Whether you are a seasoned attorney or a newbie starting in law school, someone has likely mentioned the eyebrow-raising Chewbacca defense form of legal argumentation to you.

Anyway, I'll tie this all together momentarily.

The overall notion of a Chewbacca defense is to proffer a seemingly nonsensical form of legal argument during a trial. The legal argument might be utterly fanciful and has no bearing whatsoever on the matters at hand. Some though are willing to extend the boundaries of the so-called Chewbacca defense to encompass nonsensical arguments that are within the realm of the case underway but that nonetheless makes absolutely no logical sense at all.

The origin of the named *Chewbacca defense* comes from a *South Park* episode that first aired on October 7, 1998. In this irreverent and fully cynically minded popular animated series, each episode skewers some notable element of society. The target of this cynicism for this particular episode entitled "Chef Aid" is the O.J. Simpson murder trial and the legal wrangling of attorney Johnnie Cochran (the lead lawyer for Simpson's defense team).

You certainly must know that Johnnie Cochran leveraged the courtroom act of Simpson trying on a pair of gloves retrieved from the bloody murder scene to exclaim that if the gloves don't fit then you must acquit. This became a consistent theme thereafter in the case and was a prominent point made repeatedly in his closing argument to the jury. The jury did end up voting to acquit, though how much the verbally compelling line played a demonstrative role is somewhat up to debate (well, the consensus is that the argument that "It makes no sense; it doesn't fit, if it doesn't fit you must acquit" was history-making as a legally enduring line and keystone argumentation precept).

The creators of *South Park* decided that this was a tempting target for abject sarcasm.

In the "Chef Aid' episode, a cartoon-drawn attorney resembling Cochran is defending a fictitious record company in a civil trial brought by the long-running character named Chef. The case seems to be impossible to defend against. Out of thin air and out of left field too, the Cochran character brings up an entirely non sequitur point that Chewbacca of *Star Wars* fame (per the *Return of the Jedi*) presumably lives on the planet Endor with Wookiee's, but Cochran insists that this makes no sense since Chewbacca is many times larger in size than the Wookiee's.

And if that sobering "fact" makes no sense (so he implores the jury), they must acquit the record company. The jury then rushes to "acquit" the record company, having been zombie-like convinced by this irregular and irrelevant bit of legal chicanery.

Of course, viewers and especially attorneys laugh endlessly at this whole portrayal, which is completely garbled as to what happens in civil versus criminal cases, plus has a plethora of other mistakes about the law and legal cases. No matter. The enduring worthwhile point gleaned by those immersed in the law is that sometimes the use of an outrageously non-sensical legal argument might just be the ticket to success, at times (if you don't get called out or otherwise impaled on your own petard).

The Chewbacca Way To View The Legal World

When lawyers are trying to sketch out legal arguments for a case, and if any of their colleagues come up with a floated idea that seems crazily wild and perhaps a non sequitur, it is popular to shut down the idea by merely branding it as a Chewbacca defense. During a trial, if the opposing side tries to go off the rails and make some nutty legal argument, you might instantly flash in your mind that this is an attempt to exploit a Chewbacca defense strategy (time to make a suitable objection).

As a clarification, the word "defense" does not necessarily constrain the Chewbacca approach to solely being used by the defense side of a legal case. You can readily refer to any legal argument by any side of the case as verging into the nonsensical realm of the Chewbacca defense.

Further unpacking the Chewbacca defense, you could contend that sometimes a Chewbacca defense is intentional and sometimes unintentional.

In essence, an attorney might purposely be using a non-sensical argument in hopes that it will in fact confuse or sway the jury. On the other hand, an attorney that is arguing a case in real-time might inadvertently slip into a stream of legal consciousness that comes out assuredly sounding like a Chewbacca defense (though not by design).

Shifting gears, AI-based legal reasoning systems are being devised to aid attorneys in devising legal arguments for their cases. An attorney can consult an AI system to see what kind of legal argument it recommends. In addition, a lawyer can enter their legal argument and have the AI attempt to analyze and review it, providing vital feedback to the attorney.

We probably would all agree that in the use of such AI, if an attorney had proffered a draft legal argument that seemed to be of the Chewbacca defense nature, the AI ought to warn the attorney accordingly. Better to have the AI catch this rather than being caught red-handed by the opposing side or the judge (you can perilously lose the support of the jury too).

Now then, should the AI *also* generate a Chewbacca defense line of argumentation for possible use by an attorney?

Envision that the AI has already surfaced all of the usual or normally anticipated legal arguments for the case at hand.

On top of that elucidation, perhaps the AI could go somewhat out of bounds and offer some nonsensical arguments that can be considered for your use too. It would be up to the attorney to decide whether to use those zany legal arguments or to summarily discard them, or reshape them as so desired.

Some would insist that is plainly wrong for the AI to even suggest the Chewbacca defense approach.

Why in the world would you want the AI to aid in potentially getting an attorney into hot water with the judge or the jury (a possible outcome of using a nonsensical legal argument)? Thus, AI should never propose any preposterous legal arguments.

Conclusion

The retort is that all possibilities should be considered, which a client ostensibly expects and that an attorney is obligated to seek out, and if the AI can do a little bit of Chewbacca spit-balling, so be it. The more, the better. The lawyer using the AI is the ultimate legally culpable party, and it really doesn't matter what the AI proffers.

Or, does this kind of AI venture outside the realm of what some are calling *Ethical AI* and ought to never see the light of day?

Your sense of the sensibility underlying this argument over the AI usage will have to decide whether it does or does not make sense, just as whether it makes sense for Chewbacca to be amongst the Wookiee's, a puzzling conundrum for sure.

Note: *For supplemental materials depicting the aspects discussed in this chapter, refer to Appendix B, which contains various augmented diagrams, charts, and additional related facets of relevance.*

CHAPTER 23

AI & LAW: LEGAL OPS CLOC 12

Key briefing points about this essay:

- Attorneys typically focus initially after law school on practicing law per se
- The surrounding aspects of running a law practice is not especially top of mind
- An inadequately run law practice is likely to collapse and undercut the lawyering
- Legal operations also known as Legal Ops is key, as typified by the CLOC 12 functions
- Turns out that AI applies to lawyering and all of the Legal Ops activities

Introduction

Practicing law is a tough enough task by itself, meanwhile, on top of that, the running of a law practice is an added layer of pivotal challenges and business thriving (or failing) considerations.

Underlying a law practice is a slew of essential business activities. There is ostensibly little value in putting forward your barrister proclivities if there isn't also a prudent means of ensuring that those legal beagle services will be viably run. You need to somehow find and acquire clients that you will provide services to. You will need to keep track of your billable services and ergo invoice the client accordingly (making sure that you get eventually paid, else your income will dry up).

And so on.

The point is that being a lawyer is also tantamount to being a businessperson. A wide range of so-called "administrative" tasks assuredly need to be performed for just about any law office, ranging from the solo practitioner to the vaunted auspices of BigLaw. Of course, the BigLaw and those in the middle of the size spectrum are confronted with especially thorny admin aspects based on scale. When the scale gets bigger and bigger, the administrative complexity correspondingly gets increasingly intricate and likewise significant to the daily operation of the law practice.

I put the word "administrative" into quotes because there are many lawyers that eschew the very notion of administration. To them, this is an altogether admission of a need for bureaucracy, paperwork, needless excess, and undesirable overhead, and otherwise is something that ought to be magically expunged. This kind of haughty perspective is not particularly helpful, though the cynical lawyer is apt to nonetheless make cutting and sarcastic remarks about the administrative side of a law practice.

If an inventor made a new kind of widget, they would presumably need to create a manufacturing process that would produce the widgets and get the wonderous product out the door and into the marketplace. I bring this up as somewhat of an analogy to the workings of a law office. Though the lawyers in a law practice are decidedly providing a service and not per se a product, we can aptly apply a notion of needing to operationalize the service as a cornerstone to bringing the service to the market.

Into this discourse comes the rise of legal operations or also known via the catchier catchphrase of Legal Ops.

Legal Ops aka legal operations is the entire set of operational processes, tools, people, and like elements that are at the heart of operationalizing a law practice. To be clear, lawyers are not somehow above or beyond the legal operations of a law office. Lawyers are considered an integral part of the Legal Ops efforts and there must be a seamless integration across the entire set of operationalizing portions and the act of lawyering.

When there are gaps or obstacles between the lawyering and the ops activities, you can bet that problems will arise, leading to excess costs, decreased productivity by the attorneys, foul cries of concern by clients, and altogether a mess that can undercut the best of lawyering services.

Assuming that you are reasonably convinced that there is a value-adding basis for Legal Ops, the next question might be the matter of what does Legal Ops normally consist of. I'm glad that you asked.

An especially handy and relatively popular framework for Legal Ops that embodies twelve distinctive functions is promulgated by the Corporate Legal Operations Consortium (CLOC) and has become widely known as the CLOC 12.

Here is the CLOC 12 set, listed in alphabetical order so as to emphasize that none of the functions is necessarily more important than any other. They are all important. That being said, admittedly in a given law practice some of the functions might be more extensive or elaborated than the others.

The CLOC 12 is this:

- Business Intelligence
- Financial Management
- Firm & Vendor Management
- Information Governance
- Knowledge Management
- Organization Optimization & Health
- Practice Operations
- Project/Program Management
- Service Delivery Models
- Strategic Planning
- Technology
- Training & Development

Adding To Legal Ops Is The Infusion Of AI

You might immediately have a sense of familiarity with each of the twelve functions.

For example, the odds are that any law practice in modern times has to be making use of technology, such as using computers to do legal research, prepare your case materials online, submit documents to the court, share info with your attorney colleagues, etc. The technology doesn't just run all by itself, and the odds are that you'll need some amount of tech services to keep the computers up and running.

The technology being used for lawyering is gradually becoming infused with AI capabilities. An e-Discovery tool might have a Natural Language Processing (NLP) interface akin to an Alexa or Siri that lets you ask for digital discovery searches while using somewhat everyday natural language queries. Creating a legal contract is nowadays augmented by an AI feature that can craft the contractual clauses or review clauses that you have composed.

Here's something that might surprise you and provide an added twist on the aspects of AI infusion.

Are you ready?

AI will be entering into all of the CLOC 12 functional areas. Whereas your first assumption is that the AI will only be utilized in the technology portion, the true picture is that AI is sweeping into all facets of the Legal Ops realm.

Consider as one exemplar the financial management element of Legal Ops. AI is being added to gauge patterns in financial matters such as where spending is taking place, whether budgets are sensibly prepared, and can be used to predict cash flow and the like. In short, AI is going to be part and parcel of law practices, encompassing the act of lawyering and the entirety of Legal Ops as well.

Conclusion

The logical basis for this pervasive application of AI throughout the intricate web of a law practice is imminently sensible. AI technologies are intended to imbue a semblance of intelligent-like behavior into ordinary conventional computing that is generally lacking in such capabilities.

Human activity in Legal Ops and human legal prowess leveraged in the proffering of legal services can all be boosted by a suitable dose of AI (well, making sure it is indeed suitable and well-devised AI).

Note: *For supplemental materials depicting the aspects discussed in this chapter, refer to Appendix B, which contains various augmented diagrams, charts, and additional related facets of relevance.*

CHAPTER 24
AI & LAW:
DEEP LEGAL KNOWLEDGE

Key briefing points about this essay:

- Earlier uses of AI focused on the use of rule-based expert systems and knowledge bases
- Current approaches tend to exploit Machine Learning and artificial neural networks
- A problem with Machine Learning is that it tends to be a mathematical enigma of sorts
- For topmost chess playing games, recent efforts have probed the artificial neural networks
- The same probing needs to be done with AI-based legal reasoning systems

Introduction

I have a perhaps unsettling question for you, which I hope will be taken in stride. The question revolves around how you know about the law.

Take your time, no rush needed, and stridently tell me how you know what you know about the law.

That is assuredly a mouthful and we ought to unpack it accordingly.

Notice that I didn't ask "what you know" but instead asked the pointed question of how you know the law. In short, you go to law school and learn about the law, and then you proceed into the legal practice of the law, and somehow all of that legal knowledge gets enmeshed into your mind such that you seemingly know about the law.

If I shared with you a novel legal case as a type of challenge or test, you would presumably dig deeply into that mental knowledge base about the law and come up with an answer to the legal task presented to you. I dare say that you cannot truly explain to me how your brain managed to come up with the legal answer.

Sure, you can claim that you looked closely at the particulars of the legal case. You supposedly made use of a plethora of legal rules and principles that are all ingrained in your knowledge about the law. The odds are that you would assert that via your mind you identified a variety of similar legal cases or legal precedents that were salient for the matter at hand.

And so on.

The thing is, all of that studiously boasted logical thinking is nothing more than what you *believe* has taken place in your mind. You have no *direct proof* that those mechanizations occurred. For all that we know, you made up all of that as fakery to cover for whatever really happened within your mysterious and inscrutable noggin.

What you say that your brain did is not necessarily what your brain actually did do.

It is entirely conceivable that your brain operated on a completely different basis than what you say that your mind underwent. Perhaps you've been taught since your earliest days as a growing toddler that you are to come up with a plausible cover story for what is going on inside your head. This attempt to provide a tidy explanation for your thinking has been carried forward throughout the entirety of your life.

The perhaps surprising news is that nobody can state for sure how your mind works. Sure, a lot of biological and biochemical stuff happens in the roughly 3 pounds of brain matter, yet there is little we know of how that translates into the true act of thinking. Our brains remain an enigma, even in these modern times with the amazing advances in brain scans, neuroscience breakthroughs, and the emergence of AI.

I bring up AI because one of the most vexing questions confronting the study and development of AI consists of how minds work. If we knew exactly how minds worked, the odds are that we could do a whizbang job of creating computers that would do likewise. At the same time, by taking a variety of shots at crafting AI, we might get lucky and land on an approach that turns out to be akin to how the brain functions and we'll have revealed the inner secrets of the mind.

All of this bears on the pursuit of attaining AI-based legal reasoning. The hope is that we can devise AI that will perform legal reasoning on par with that of human lawyers. One means of reaching that aspirational goal would be to build AI legal reasoner systems and see if they rise to the proficiency of human attorneys.

Inside Those AI-Based Legal Reasoners

Prior approaches to designing and constructing AI-based legal reasoning tended to use a rules-based or expert systems approach. This is also commonly known as using a knowledge base for the formulation of an artificial reasoning system. Briefly, you identify or layout a slew of rules, somewhat similar to If-Then types of elaborations, and you toss them into a large bucket of such rules. The rules then are applied via the computer system and voila, hopefully, a veneer of legal reasoning arises.

The latest approaches shift direction and tend to make use of artificial neural networks. These are highly simplified simulation-like computer models that seek to replicate the biological elements typified by neurons in the brain.

Please realize that these artificial neural networks are a far cry from the real thing and the wetware bona fide brain is lightyears ahead of these computer-based versions.

In any case, the use of Machine Learning or also known as Deep Learning will oftentimes use artificial neural networks. One issue about this is that the result is a morass of mathematical interconnections that do not lend themselves to being readily logically explained. How do all of those calculations and computational artifacts end up ostensibly being able to attain a semblance of intelligent-like results?

The same kind of question can be asked about the advances made in computerized chess playing. You see, the amazing push forward on having computer chess-playing that can exceed the topmost chess masters can be greatly attributed to the shift toward using Machine Learning and artificial neural networks.

An intriguing question is whether the morass of mathematical artificial neural networks has somehow landed onto the logical rules that we humans believe are the key to intelligent behavior, which in the use case of chess would be the well-known articulated chess strategies.

A fascinating study of presumed knowledge within a topmost chess-playing system called AlphaZero mentions this quest: "Machine learning systems are commonly believed to learn opaque, uninterpretable representations that have little in common with human understanding of the domain they are trained on. Recently, however, empirical evidence has suggested that at least in some cases neural networks learn human-understandable representations. Notable examples include single neurons in a classifier corresponding to mountain tops or snow, syntactic information in language models, surprisingly sophisticated conceptual representations in a multimodal network emerging from the alignment of visual and textual data, and the wide range of findings in the growing field of BERTology" (as indicated in a research paper entitled "Acquisition Of Chess Knowledge In AlphaZero" by Thomas McGrath, Andrei Kapishnikov, Nenad Toma, Adam Pearce, Demis Hassabis, Been Kim, Ulrich Paquet, and Vladimir Kramnik, 2021).

By probing into the artificial neural network, the researchers sought to discover whether various human-assumed chess concepts, rules, and strategies could be reverse-engineered out of the mathematical and computational quagmire. For those of you familiar with chess, the belief was that encoded into the web of AlphaZero would be aspects such as a passed pawn, or the connecting of rooks, or the importance of controlling an open file (chessboard row), etc.

Based on the analysis and the use of concept regression findings, they tentatively concluded that there does appear to be human-interpretable factors within the otherwise arcane and inscrutable system.

Conclusion

This brings us to the doorstep of AI-based legal reasoning systems. Those artificial legal reasoners that are being constructed via Machine Learning and utilizing artificial neural networks could likewise leverage the same computational probing activities to try and discern whether venerated legal concepts and legal rules are arising within the deep recesses of the AI.

We presumably might divine that the computational approach is landing on the same logic-based explicit legal rules that we all ordinarily accept at face value. Imagine the surprise to discover that either this is not the case, or that there is an entirely different form or dimension of legal reasoning that we have been unaware of this entire time.

That would be quite a wee bit of a head spinner, legally speaking.

Note: *For supplemental materials depicting the aspects discussed in this chapter, refer to Appendix B, which contains various augmented diagrams, charts, and additional related facets of relevance.*

CHAPTER 25

AI & LAW: SUPERHUMAN AI

Key briefing points about this essay:

- The catchphrase of being superhuman has crept into our everyday lexicon
- Part of this emergence is due to the advent of modern-day AI systems
- When an AI system seems to have exceeded human capacities, it gets the superhuman title
- Turns out that there is no accepted common definition for the superhuman AI notion
- We are woefully witnessing increasing claims of so-called superhuman AI-based lawyering

Introduction

You might be the kind of lawyer that has been referred to as a superstar attorney (if so, kudos to you).

That being said, are you also a superhuman attorney?

This is not just a piece of whimsy. The notion of being superhuman has risen in popularity over the last several years as AI has increasingly been infused into today's software. We are often told that some AI-infused application has reached superhuman achievements.

There are lots of problems inherent in making such outsized claims.

First, nobody can definitely say and nor agree on what the characteristics of AI being "superhuman" consist of. Those of us immersed in the field of law are well aware that the meaning of words is crucial to discourse and can at times be a legally tremendous consideration. For example, legal cases are replete with wrangling's over the word "is" or the word "was" as to the particular semantic indication that such words convey (you might recall the historical focus on those two words in the famous or shall it be said infamous denial by President Clinton).

Second, the notion of superhuman does not seem to equate to other more commonly accepted and reasonably utilized wordings such as superstar or super-duper. We are readily willing to accept the idea that someone is a superstar, suggesting that they are at the top of their game, as it were. Still, this denotes that their performance is merely in line with what other people have or can do, and ostensibly ranks somewhere in the topmost level.

Third, superhuman would seem to imply that someone or something is beyond that which humans can achieve. This raises a bit of a paradox when it comes to speaking about humans. You see, if a human is said to be superhuman, this is an obvious contradiction if they are in fact a human. A human is a human, and thus superhuman-like behavior should be reclassified as being within the class of human when it is attributed to an actual human.

If tomorrow we woke up and an otherwise unaided human could run faster than a speeding bullet and could leap over tall buildings in a single bound, it seems doubtful that this kind of entity that performed such a feat is within the category of humanoids.

The odds are that we would all concede that the thing doing this amazing display would be superhuman, assuming that in all other respects we are willing to ascribe a semblance of being human to the creature of attention.

The point here is that you could otherwise presumably and oddly refer to a car as being superhuman if you wanted to do so. A car goes much faster than any unaided human. Ergo, a car is superhuman. Few would be arguing in favor of that rather farfetched notion. A car is not at all like a human in any reasonable manner of speaking. Trying to assign the superhuman label seems patently akilter.

This brings us to the doorstep of AI.

Researchers and the media have become enamored of anointing all sorts of AI systems as being so-called superhuman. This certainly is eye-catching and can garner tons of views and readership. Unfortunately, it is also false, misleading, and ought to be criticized and called out for the insidious and deceptive meaning this conveys.

As they say, there ought to be a law about this.

Making Sensible The Superhuman AI Sensibility

Let's unpack an example of how the superhuman moniker is typically used in an AI context.

A chess-playing program that uses various AI techniques and technologies is able to beat many chess players. Suppose we have the highest-ranking human chess grandmaster compete with this chess-playing program. Out of several matches in a chess tournament, the AI-based chess program wins decidedly.

Voila, the headlines proclaim that this chess-playing AI system is superhuman.

Is it?

Keep in mind that this chess program is solely devoted to the playing of chess. It cannot even balance your checkbook and nor can it sing a song. Insiders would tend to declare that it is a form of *narrow AI*, designed and built to perform a singular kind of task. This is assuredly not considered Artificial General Intelligence (AGI), which is the grand aspiration for having AI that can perform general tasks that humans can perform. The AI lacks any semblance of common sense reasoning, it is not at all anywhere close to embodying sentience, and so on.

To refer to the chess-playing AI program as superhuman would be an anthropomorphic overreach.

There is really nothing at all about this chess program that fits the description of a humanoid. We could likely make a logic leap that a car is as much akin to a human as is this chess-playing program.

Shifting gears, you need to prepare yourself for the kinds of superhuman claims that are going to arise in the domain of AI and the law.

A program using AI capabilities is able to computationally analyze the text of a contract and find portions that seem to be legally questionable. An attorney would find this a handy tool. Does this AI-based program get to be referred to as superhuman in terms of what it provides? I dare suggest that doing so is an outrageous overstatement.

Well, what would be a superhuman lawyering capability?

If an AI system could do legal reasoning that encompassed all the laws of the US and included all the state laws too, we might be tempted to lean toward the aspect that this seems superhuman. Presumably, no human could in their heads retain all such laws.

If an AI system doing legal reasoning could produce legal arguments that no humans have ever devised, we might nod our heads and accede that this appears to be superhuman lawyering.

Of course, we might not be able to predict what that winning legal argument is, since we are limited by our being human and the superhuman goes beyond our conventional human reasoning per se.

Conclusion

I realize that there are those that would argue that this whole argument about *superhuman* as a properly or improperly used anointer is unworthy of attention. They would say that the superhuman label is simply a shortcut and a loquaciously fanciful way to describe something. Nobody takes it seriously, they would vehemently claim.

I'm counting the days until a legal case makes its way into our courts and we get a ruling on the legally binding nature of proclaiming that an AI system is allegedly superhuman. This will potentially shake up those that relish doting the superhuman label on whatever they please.

One must ponder, perhaps a superhuman lawyer will be needed to make the case for what truly constitutes superhuman AI, and maybe that superhuman lawyer will actually be a superhuman AI-infused robo-lawyer.

.

Note: *For supplemental materials depicting the aspects discussed in this chapter, refer to Appendix B, which contains various augmented diagrams, charts, and additional related facets of relevance.*

APPENDIX A
TEACHING WITH THIS MATERIAL AND BIBLIOGRAPHY

The essays in this book can readily be used as a reading supplemental to augment traditional textbook-oriented content, particularly used in a class on AI or a class about the law.

Courses where this material is most likely applicable encompass classes at a college or university level.

Here are some typical settings that might apply:

- Computer Science. Classes studying AI, or possibly a CS social impacts class, etc.

- Law. Law classes exploring technology and its adoption for legal uses.

- Sociology. Sociology classes on the adoption and advancement of technology.

Specialized classes at the undergraduate and graduate level can also make use of this material.

For each chapter, consider whether you think the chapter provides material relevant to your course topic.

There are plenty of opportunities to get the students thinking about the topics and encourage them to decide whether they agree or disagree with the points offered and positions taken.

I would also encourage you to have the students do additional research beyond the chapter material presented (I provide next some suggested assignments that they can do).

RESEARCH ASSIGNMENTS ON THESE TOPICS

Your students can find research and background material on these topics, doing so in various tech journals, law journals, and other related publications.

Here are some suggestions for homework or projects that you could assign to students:

a) Assignment for foundational AI research topics: Research and prepare a paper and a presentation on a specific aspect of AI, such as Machine Learning, ANN, etc. The paper should cite at least 3 reputable sources. Compare and contrast to what has been stated in the chosen chapter.

b) Assignment for Law topics: Research and prepare a paper covering Law aspects via at least 3 reputable sources and analyze the characterizations. Compare and contrast to what has been stated in the chosen chapter.

c) Assignment for a Business topic: Research and prepare a paper and a presentation on businesses and advanced technology regarding AI and Law. What is trending, and why? Make sure to cite at least 3 reputable sources. Compare and contrast to the depictions herein.

d) Assignment to do a Startup: Have the students prepare a paper or business plan about how they might start up a business in this realm. They could also be asked to present their business plan and should also have a prepared presentation deck to coincide with it.

You can certainly adjust the aforementioned assignments to fit your particular needs and class structure.

You'll notice that I usually suggest that (at least) 3 reputable cited sources be utilized for the paper writing-based assignments.

I usually steer students toward "reputable" publications, since otherwise, they will cite some less reliable sources that have little or no credentials, other than that they happened to appear online was easy to retrieve. You can, of course, define "reputable" in whatever way you prefer, for example, some faculty think Wikipedia is not reputable while others believe it is reputable and allow students to cite it.

The reason that I usually ask for at least 3 citations is that if the student only relies upon one or two citations, they usually settle on whatever they happened to find the fastest. By requiring 3 (or more) citations, it usually seems to inspire them to explore more extensively and likely end-up finding five or more sources, and then whittling it down to 3 if so needed.

I have not specified the length of their papers and leave that to you to tell the students what you prefer.

For each of those assignments, you could end up with a short one to two-pager or you could do a dissertation length in-depth paper. Base the length on whatever best fits for your class, and likewise the credit amount of the assignment within the context of the other grading metrics you'll be using for the class.

I usually try to get students to present their work, in addition to doing the writing. This is a helpful practice for what they will do in the business world. Most of the time, they will be required to prepare an analysis and present it. If you don't have the class time or inclination to have the students present their papers, then you can presumably omit the aspect of them putting together presentations.

GUIDE TO USING THE CHAPTERS

For each of the chapters, I provide the next some various ways to use the chapter contents.

You can assign the below tasks as individual homework assignments, or the tasks can be used for team projects. You can easily layout a series of assignments, such as indicating that the students are to do item "a" below for say Chapter 1, then "b" for the next chapter of the book, and so on.

a) What is the main point of the chapter and describe in your own words the significance of the topic.

b) Identify at least two aspects in the chapter that you agree with and support your concurrence by providing at least one other outside researched item as support; make sure to explain your basis for agreeing with the aspects.

c) Identify at least two aspects in the chapter that you disagree with and support your disagreement by providing at least one other outside researched item as support; make sure to explain your basis for disagreeing with the aspects.

d) Find an aspect that was not covered extensively in the chapter, doing so by conducting outside research, and then offer an expanded indication about how that aspect ties into the chapter, along with the added significance it brings to the topic.

e) Interview a specialist in the industry about the topic of the chapter, collect from them their thoughts and opinions, and readdress the chapter by citing your source and how they compared and contrasted to the material,

f) Interview a relevant professor or researcher in a college or university setting about the topic of the chapter, collect from them their thoughts and opinions, and readdress the chapter by citing your source and how they compared and contrasted to the material,

g) Try to update a chapter by finding out the latest on the topic and ascertain whether the issue or topic has now been solved or whether it is still being addressed, explain what you come up with.

The above are all ways in which you can get the students of your class involved in considering the material of a given chapter. You could mix things up by having one of those above assignments per each week, covering the chapters over the course of the semester or quarter.

SUGGESTED REFERENCES TO EXPLORE

To help get your students started in finding relevant and important papers on the topic of AI and the law, I provide next a handy bibliography that can be utilized.

You could also assign the students to each (or in teams) read an assigned reference from the list, and then have them provide either a written summary and review or do so as part of a classroom presentation.

BIBLIOGRAPHIC REFERENCES

1. Aleven, Vincent (1997). "Teaching Case-Based Argumentation Through a Model and Examples," Ph.D. Dissertation, University of Pittsburgh.

2. Aleven, Vincent (2003). "Using Background Knowledge in Case-Based Legal Reasoning: A Computational Model and an Intelligent Learning Environment," Artificial Intelligence.

3. Amgoud, Leila (2012). "Five Weaknesses of ASPIC+," Volume 299, Communications in Computer and Information Science (CCIS).

4. Antonious, Grigoris, and George Baryannis, Sotiris Batsakis, Guido Governatori, Livio Robaldo, Givoanni Siragusa, Ilias Tachmazidis (2018). "Legal Reasoning and Big Data: Opportunities and Challenges," August 2018, MIREL Workshop on Mining and Reasoning Legal Texts.

5. Ashley, Kevin (1991). "Reasoning with Cases and Hypotheticals in HYPO," Volume 34, International Journal of Man-Machine Studies.

6. Ashley, Kevin, and Karl Branting, Howard Margolis, and Cass Sunstein (2001). "Legal Reasoning and Artificial Intelligence: How Computers 'Think' Like Lawyers," Symposium: Legal Reasoning and Artificial Intelligence, University of Chicago Law School Roundtable.

7. Baker, Jamie (2018). "A Legal Research Odyssey: Artificial Intelligence as Disrupter," Law Library Journal.

8. Batsakis, Sotiris, and George Baryannis, Guido Governatori, Illias Tachmazidis, Grigoris Antoniou (2018). "Legal Representation and Reasoning in Practice: A Critical Comparison," Volume 313, Legal Knowledge and Information Systems.

9. Bench-Capon, Trevor (2004). "AGATHA: Automation of the Construction of Theories in Case Law Domains," January 2004, Legal Knowledge and Information Systems Jurix 2004, Amsterdam.

10. Bench-Capon, Trevor (2012). "Representing Popov v Hayashi with Dimensions and Factors," March 2012, Artificial Intelligence and Law.

11. Bench-Capon, Trevor, and Givoanni Sartor (2003). "A Model of Legal Reasoning with Cases Incorporating Theories and Values," November 2013, Artificial Intelligence.

12. Breuker, Joost (1996). "A Functional Ontology of Law," October 1996, ResearchGate.

13. Bruninghaus, Stefanie, and Kevin Ashley (2003). "Combining Case-Based and Model-Based Reasoning for Predicting the Outcome of Legal Cases," June 2003, ICCBR'03: Proceedings of the 5th International Conference on Case-based reasoning: Research and Development.

14. Buchanan, Bruce, and Thomas Headrick (1970). "Some Speculation about Artificial Intelligence and Legal Reasoning," Volume 23, Stanford Law Review.

15. Chagal-Feferkorn, Karni (2019). "Am I An Algorithm or a Product: When Products Liability Should Apply to Algorithmic Decision-Makers," Stanford Law & Policy Review.

16. Douglas, William (1948). "The Dissent: A Safeguard of Democracy," Volume 32, Journal of the American Judicature Society.

17. Dung, P, and R. Kowalski, F. Toni (2006). "Dialectic Proof Procedures for Assumption-Based Admissible Argumentation," Artificial Intelligence.

18. Eliot, Lance (2020). AI And Legal Reasoning Essentials. LBE Press Publishing.

19. Eliot, Lance (2020). Artificial Intelligence and LegalTech Essentials. LBE Press Publishing.

20. Eliot, Lance (2020). "FutureLaw 2020 Showcases How Tech is Transforming The Law, Including the Impacts of AI," April 16, 2020, Forbes.

21. Erdem, Esra, and Michael Gelfond, Nicola Leone (2016). "Applications of Answer Set Programming," AI Magazine.

22. Gardner, Anne (1987). Artificial Intelligence and Legal Reasoning. MIT Press.

23. Genesereth, Michael (2009). "Computational Law: The Cop in the Backseat," Stanford Center for Legal Informatics, Stanford University.

24. Ghosh, Mirna (2019). "Automation of Legal Reasoning and Decision Based on Ontologies," Normandie Universite.

25. Grabmair, Matthias (2017). "Predicting Trade Secret Case Outcomes using Argument Schemes and Learned Quantitative Value Effect Tradeoffs," IJCAI June 12, 2017, London, United Kingdom.

26. Hage, Jaap (1996). "A Theory of Legal Reasoning and a Logic to Match," Volume 4, Artificial Intelligence and Law.

27. Hage, Jaap (2000). "Dialectical Models in Artificial Intelligence and Law," Artificial Intelligence and Law.

28. Hage, Japp, and Ronald Leenes, Arno Lodder (1993). "Hard Cases: A Procedural Approach," Artificial Intelligence and Law.

29. Hobbes, Thomas (1651). The Matter, Form, and Power of a Common-Wealth Ecclesiasticall and Civil.

30. Holmes, Oliver (1897). "The Path of the Law," Volume 10, Harvard Law Review.

31. Katz, Daniel, and Michael Bommarito, Josh Blackman (2017). "A General Approach for Predicting the Behavior of the Supreme Court of the United States," April 12, 2017, PLOS ONE.

32. Kowalski, Robert, and Francesca Toni (1996). "Abstract Argumentation," AI-Law96.

33. Laswell, Harold (1955). "Current Studies of the Decision Process: Automation Creativity," Volume 8, Western Political Quarterly.

34. Libal, Tomer, and Alexander Steen (2019). "The NAI Suite: Drafting and Reasoning over Legal Texts," October 15, 2019, arXiv.

35. Lipton, Zachary (2017). "The Mythos of Model Interpretability," March 6, 2017, arXiv.

36. Martin, Andrew, and Kevin Quinn, Theodore Ruger, Pauline Kim (2004). "Competing Approaches to Predicting Supreme Court Decision Making," December 2014, Symposium on Forecasting U.S. Supreme Court Decisions.

37. McCarty, Thorne (1977). "Reflections on TAXMAN: An Experiment in Artificial Intelligence and Legal Reasoning," January 1977, Harvard Law Review.

38. Modgil, Sanjay, and Henry Prakken (2013). "The ASPIC+ Framework for Structured Argumentation: A Tutorial," December 16, 2013, Argument & Computation.

39. Mowbray, Andrew, and Philip Chung, Graham Greenleaf (2019). "Utilising AI in the Legal Assistance Sector," LegalAIIA Workshop, ICAIL, June 17, 2019, Montreal, Canada.

40. Parasuraman, Raja, and Thomas Sheridan, Christopher Wickens (2000). "A Model for Types and Levels of Human Interaction with Automation," May 2000, IEEE Transactions on Systems, Man, and Cybernetics.

41. Popple, James (1993). "SHYSTER: A Pragmatic Legal Expert System," Ph.D. Dissertation, Australian National University.

42. Prakken, Henry, and Giovanni Sartor (2015). "Law and Logic: A Review from an Argumentation Perspective," Volume 227, Artificial Intelligence.

43. Rissland, Edwina (1988). Artificial Intelligence and Legal Reasoning: A Discussion of the Field and Gardner's Book," Volume 9, AI Magazine.

44. Rissland, Edwina (1990). "Artificial Intelligence and Law: Stepping Stones to a Model of Legal Reasoning," Yale Law Journal.

45. Searle, John (1980). "Minds, Brains, and Programs," Volume 3, Behavioral and Brain Sciences.

46. Sunstein, Cass (2001). "Of Artificial Intelligence and Legal Reasoning," University of Chicago Law School, Public Law and Legal Theory Working Papers.

47. Sunstein, Cass, and Kevin Ashley, Karl Branting, Howard Margolis (2001). "Legal Reasoning and Artificial Intelligence: How Computers 'Think' Like Lawyers," Symposium: Legal Reasoning and Artificial Intelligence, University of Chicago Law School Roundtable.

48. Surden, Harry (2014). "Machine Learning and Law," Washington Law Review.

49. Surden, Harry (2019). "Artificial Intelligence and Law: An Overview," Summer 2019, Georgia State University Law Review.

50. Valente, Andre, and Joost Breuker (1996). "A Functional Ontology of Law," Artificial Intelligence and Law.

51. Waltl, Bernhard, and Roland Vogl (2018). "Explainable Artificial Intelligence: The New Frontier in Legal Informatics," February 2018, Jusletter IT 22, Stanford Center for Legal Informatics, Stanford University.

52. Wittgenstein, Ludwig (1953). Philosophical Investigations. Blackwell Publishing.

APPENDIX B
SUPPLEMENTAL FIGURES AND CHARTS

For the convenience of viewing, supplemental figures and charts related to the topics discussed are shown on the next pages

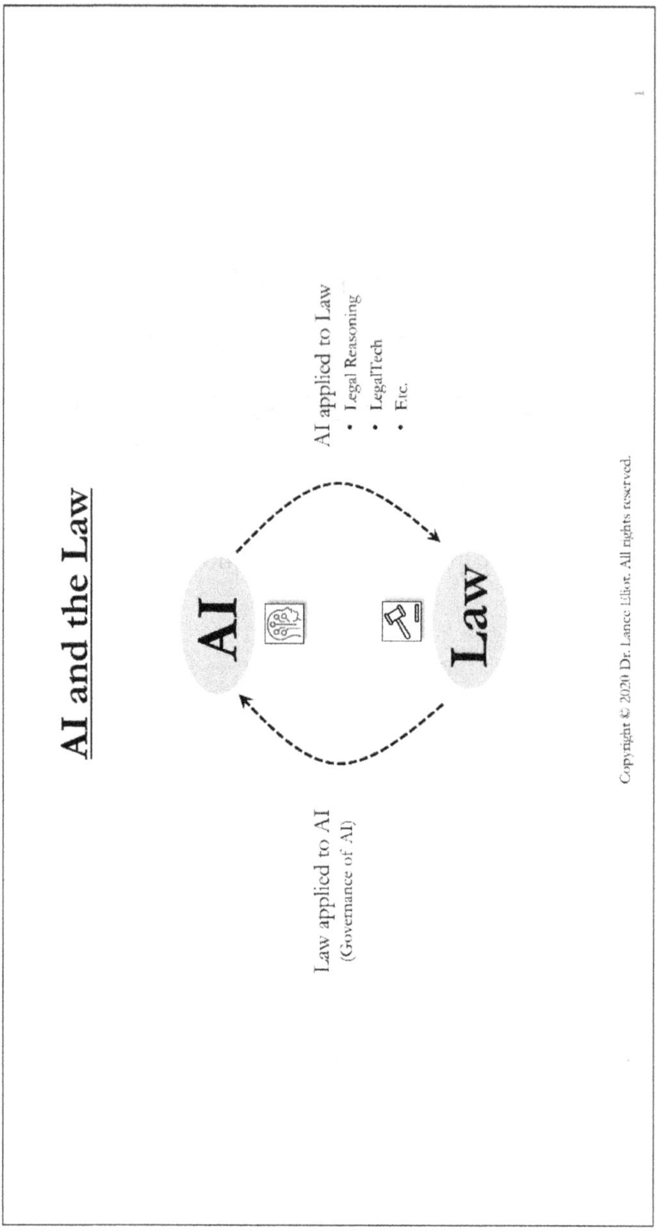
AI and the Law
AI
Law
AI applied to Law
• Legal Reasoning
• LegalTech
• Etc.
Law applied to AI
(Governance of AI)
Copyright © 2020 Dr. Lance Eliot. All rights reserved.
1

Figure 1

AI & Law: Levels of Autonomy For AI Legal Reasoning (AILR)

Level	Descriptor	Examples	Automation	Status
0	No Automation	Manual, paper-based (no automation)	None	De Facto - In Use
1	Simple Assistance Automation	Word Processing, XLS, online legal docs, etc.	Legal Assist	Widely In Use
2	Advanced Assistance Automation	Query-style NLP, ML for case prediction, etc.	Legal Assist	Some In Use
3	Semi-Autonomous Automation	KBS & ML/DL for legal reasoning & analysis, etc.	Legal Assist	Primarily Prototypes & Research Based
4	AILR Domain Autonomous	Versed only in a specific legal domain	Legal Advisor (law fluent)	None As Yet
5	AILR Fully Autonomous	Versatile within and across all legal domains	Legal Advisor (law fluent)	None As Yet
6	AILR Superhuman Autonomous	Exceeds human-based legal reasoning	Supra Legal Advisor	Indeterminate

Figure 1: AI & Law - Autonomous Levels by Rows

Source Author: Dr. Lance B. Eliot

V1.3

Figure 2

AI & Law: Levels of Autonomy For AI Legal Reasoning (AILR)

	Level 0	Level 1	Level 2	Level 3	Level 4	Level 5	Level 6
Descriptor	No Automation	Simple Assistance Automation	Advanced Assistance Automation	Semi-Autonomous Automation	AILR Domain Autonomous	AILR Fully Autonomous	AILR Superhuman Autonomous
Examples	Manual, paper-based (no automation)	Word Processing, XLS, online legal docs, etc.	Query-style NLP, ML for case prediction, etc.	KBS & ML/DL for legal reasoning & analysis, etc.	Versed only in a specific legal domain	Versatile within and across all legal domains	Exceeds human-based legal reasoning
Automation	None	Legal Assist	Legal Assist	Legal Assist	Legal Advisor (law fluent)	Legal Advisor (law fluent)	Supra Legal Advisor
Status	De Facto – In Use	Widely In Use	Some In Use	Primarily Prototypes & Research-based	None As Yet	None As Yet	Indeterminate

Figure 2: AI & Law - Autonomous Levels by Columns

Source Author: Dr. Lance B. Eliot

V1.3

Figure 3

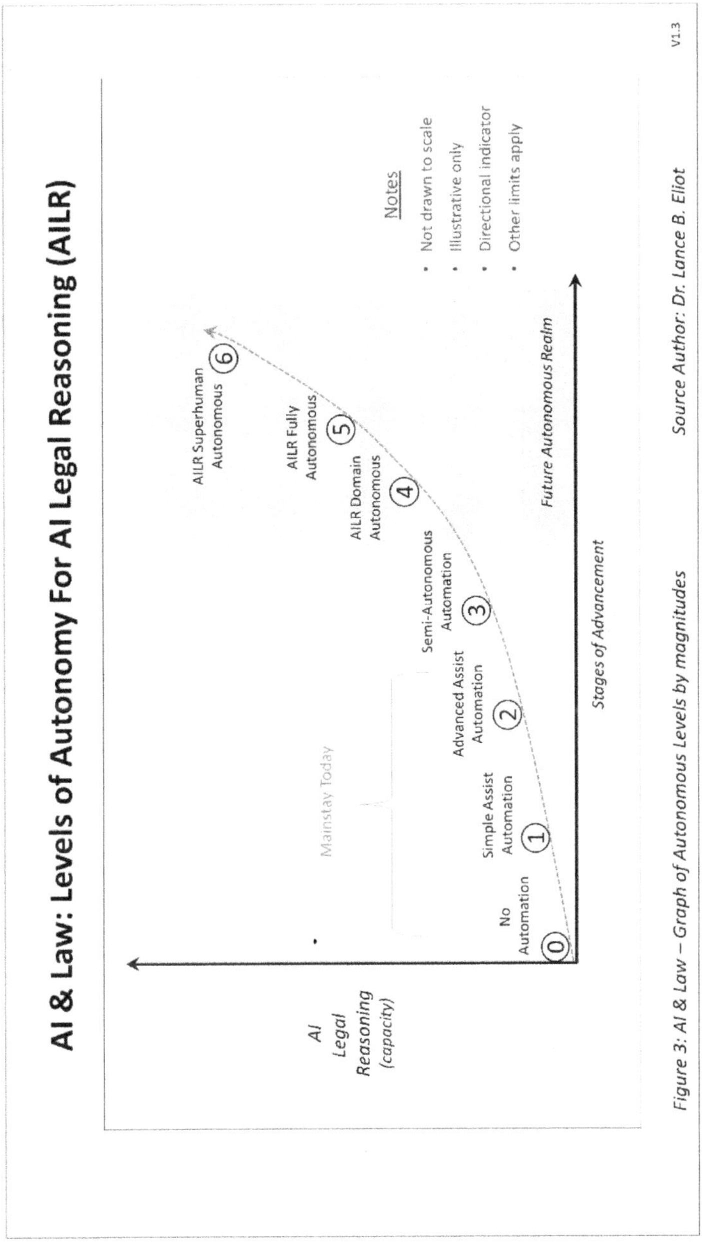
AI & Law: Levels of Autonomy For AI Legal Reasoning (AILR)
AI Legal Reasoning (capacity)
0 No Automation
1 Simple Assist Automation
2 Advanced Assist Automation
3 Semi-Autonomous Automation
4 AILR Domain Autonomous
5 AILR Fully Autonomous
6 AILR Superhuman Autonomous
Mainstay Today
Stages of Advancement
Future Autonomous Realm
Notes
Not drawn to scale
Illustrative only
Directional indicator
Other limits apply
Figure 3: AI & Law – Graph of Autonomous Levels by magnitudes
Source Author: Dr. Lance B. Eliot
V1.3

Figure 4

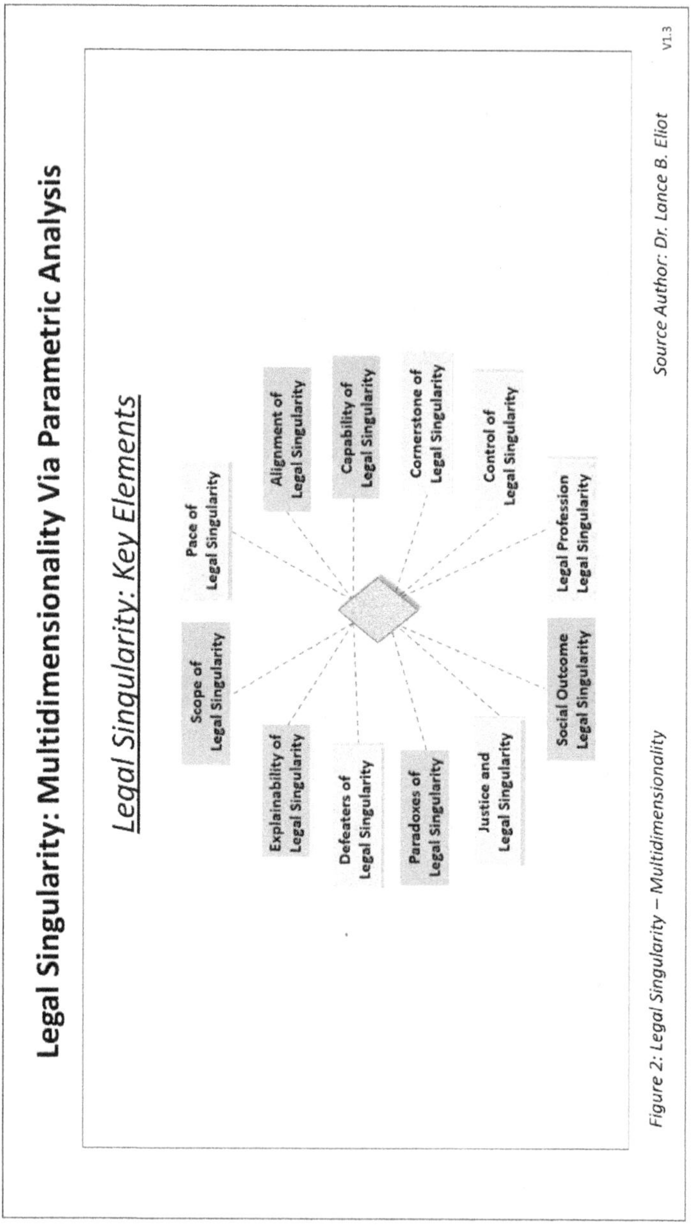
Legal Singularity: Multidimensionality Via Parametric Analysis
Legal Singularity: Key Elements
Scope of Legal Singularity
Pace of Legal Singularity
Explainability of Legal Singularity
Alignment of Legal Singularity
Defeaters of Legal Singularity
Capability of Legal Singularity
Paradoxes of Legal Singularity
Cornerstone of Legal Singularity
Justice and Legal Singularity
Control of Legal Singularity
Social Outcome Legal Singularity
Legal Profession Legal Singularity
Figure 2: Legal Singularity – Multidimensionality
Source Author: Dr. Lance B. Eliot
V1.3

Figure 5

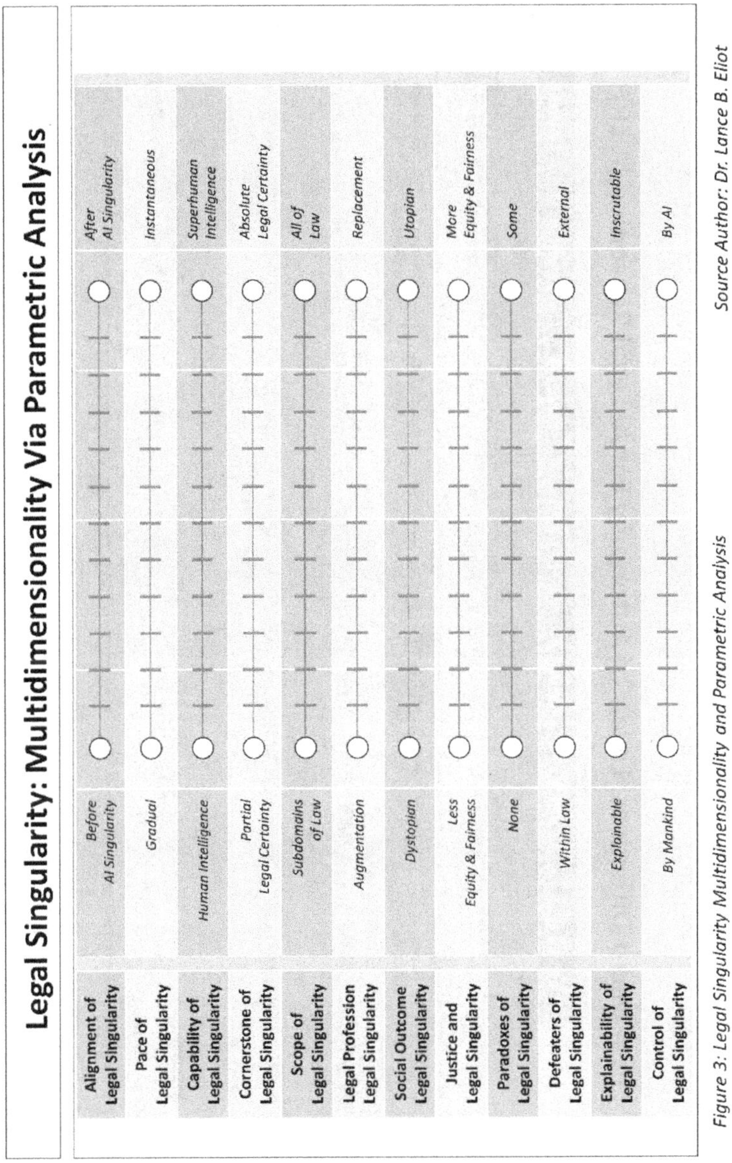
Legal Singularity: Multidimensionality Via Parametric Analysis
Alignment of Legal Singularity
Before AI Singularity
After AI Singularity
Pace of Legal Singularity
Gradual
Instantaneous
Capability of Legal Singularity
Human Intelligence
Superhuman Intelligence
Cornerstone of Legal Singularity
Partial Legal Certainty
Absolute Legal Certainty
Scope of Legal Singularity
Subdomains of Law
All of Law
Legal Profession Legal Singularity
Augmentation
Replacement
Social Outcome Legal Singularity
Dystopian
Utopian
Justice and Legal Singularity
Less Equity & Fairness
More Equity & Fairness
Paradoxes of Legal Singularity
None
Some
Defeaters of Legal Singularity
Within Law
External
Explainability of Legal Singularity
Explainable
Inscrutable
Control of Legal Singularity
By Mankind
By AI
Figure 3: Legal Singularity Multidimensionality and Parametric Analysis
Source Author: Dr. Lance B. Eliot

Figure 6

Legal Micro-Directives: Levels of Autonomy For AI Legal Reasoning (AILR)

	Level 0	Level 1	Level 2	Level 3	Level 4	Level 5	Level 6
Descriptor	No Automation	Simple Assistance Automation	Advanced Assistance Automation	Semi-Autonomous Automation	AILR Domain Autonomous	AILR Fully Autonomous	AILR Superhuman Autonomous
Examples	Manual, paper-based (no automation)	Word Processing, XLS, online legal docs, etc.	Query-style NLP, ML for case prediction, etc.	KBS & ML/DL for legal reasoning & analysis, etc.	Versed only in a specific legal domain	Versatile within and across all legal domains	Exceeds human-based legal reasoning
Automation	None	Legal Assist	Legal Assist	Legal Assist	Legal Advisor (law fluent)	Legal Advisor (law fluent)	Supra Legal Advisor
Status	De Facto – In Use	Widely In Use	Some In Use	Primarily Prototypes & Research-based	None As Yet	None As Yet	Indeterminate
AI-Enabled Legal Micro-Directives	*n/a*	*Impractical*	*Incubatory*	*Infancy*	*Narrow*	*Wide*	*Consummate*

Figure 1: Legal Micro-Directives - Autonomous Levels of AILR by Columns

Source Author: Dr. Lance B. Eliot

V1.3

Figure 7

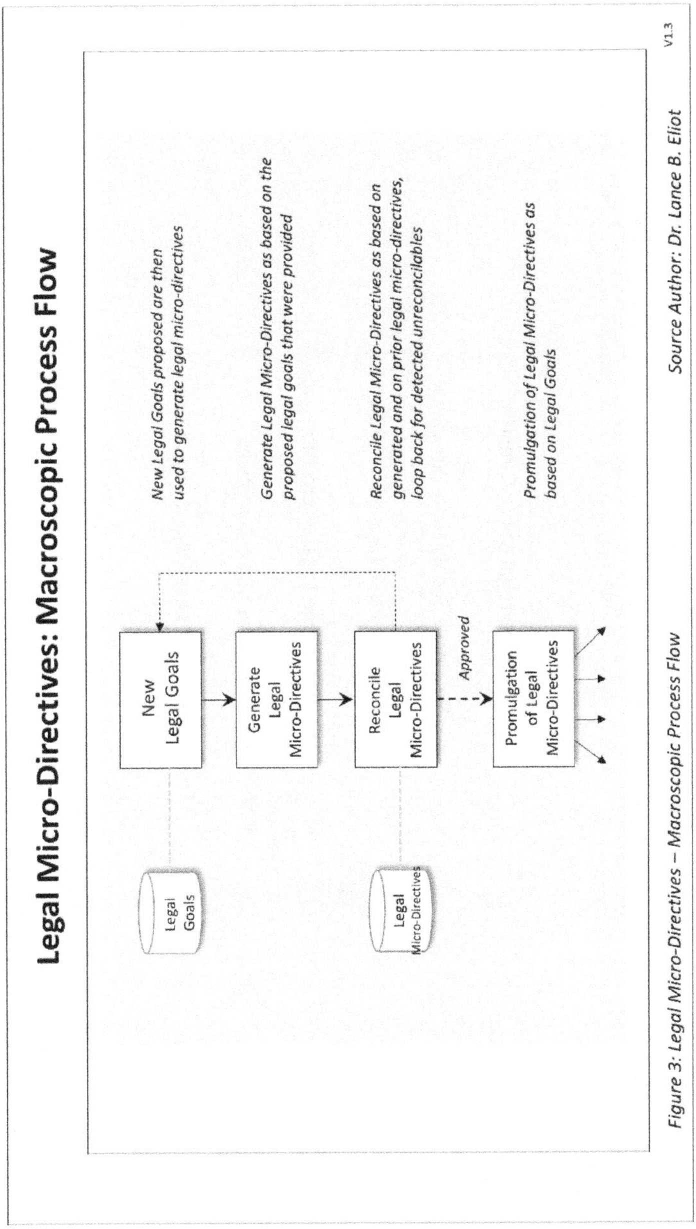
Legal Micro-Directives: Macroscopic Process Flow
Legal Goals
Legal Micro-Directives
New Legal Goals
Generate Legal Micro-Directives
Reconcile Legal Micro-Directives
Approved
Promulgation of Legal Micro-Directives
New Legal Goals proposed are then used to generate legal micro-directives
Generate Legal Micro-Directives as based on the proposed legal goals that were provided
Reconcile Legal Micro-Directives as based on generated and on prior legal micro-directives, loop back for detected unreconcilables
Promulgation of Legal Micro-Directives as based on Legal Goals
Figure 3: Legal Micro-Directives – Macroscopic Process Flow
Source Author: Dr. Lance B. Eliot
V1.3

Figure 8

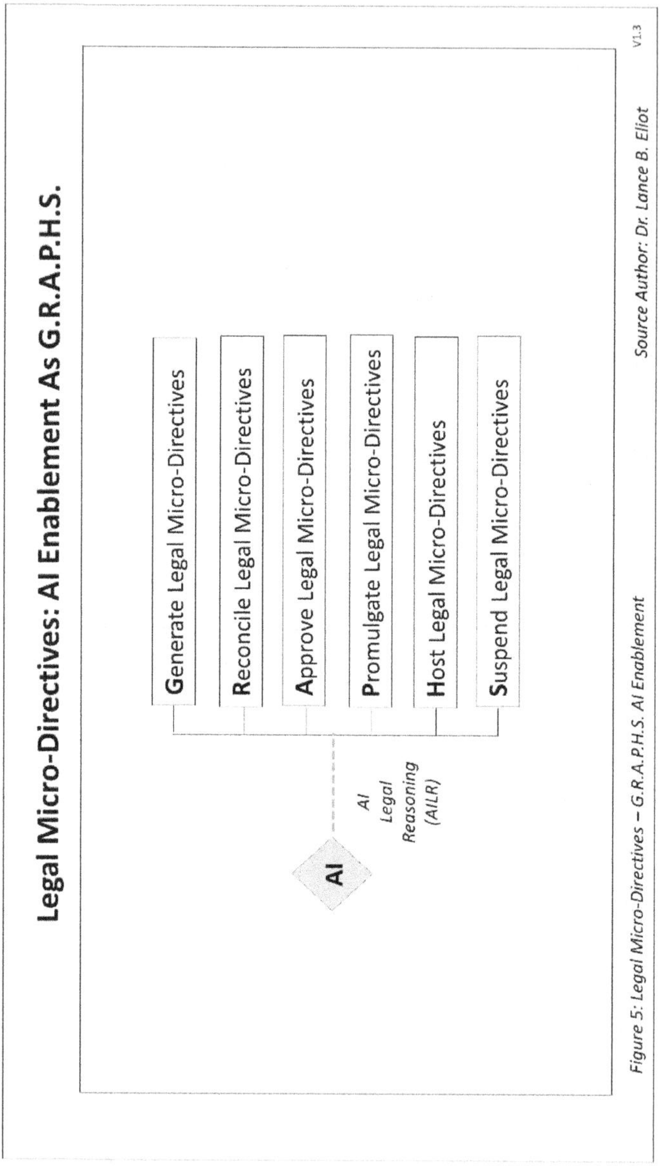
Legal Micro-Directives: AI Enablement As G.R.A.P.H.S.
AI
AI Legal Reasoning (AILR)
Generate Legal Micro-Directives
Reconcile Legal Micro-Directives
Approve Legal Micro-Directives
Promulgate Legal Micro-Directives
Host Legal Micro-Directives
Suspend Legal Micro-Directives
Figure 5: Legal Micro-Directives – G.R.A.P.H.S. AI Enablement
Source Author: Dr. Lance B. Eliot
V1.3

Figure 9

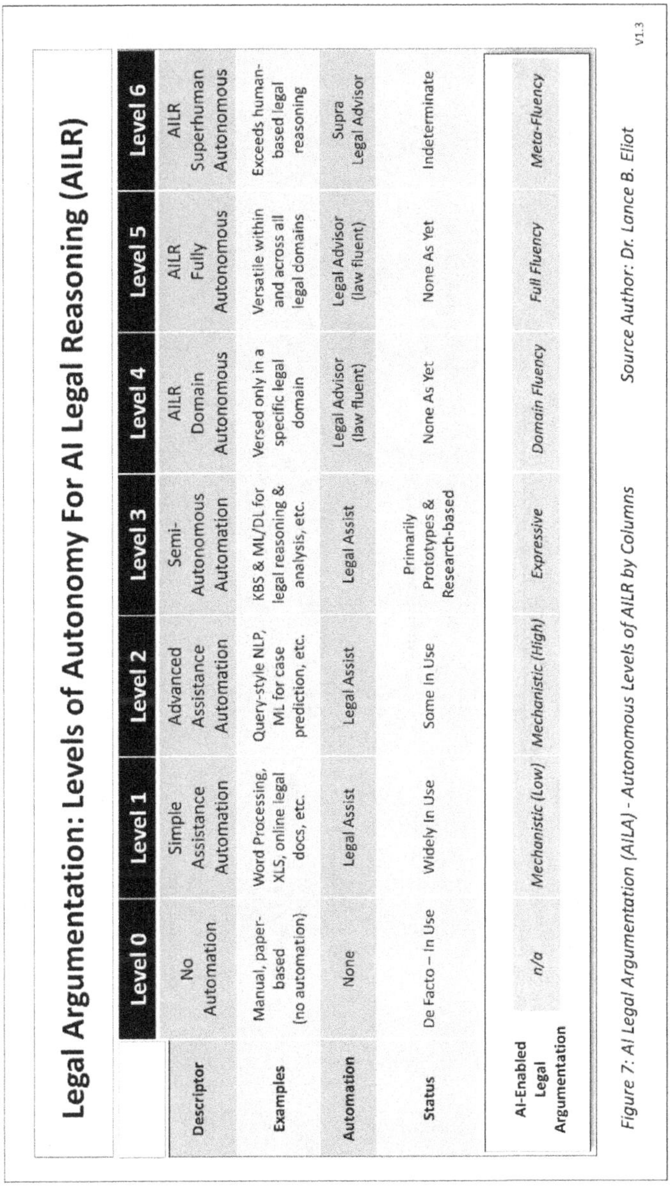

Legal Argumentation: Levels of Autonomy For AI Legal Reasoning (AILR)

	Level 0	Level 1	Level 2	Level 3	Level 4	Level 5	Level 6
Descriptor	No Automation	Simple Assistance Automation	Advanced Assistance Automation	Semi-Autonomous Automation	AILR Domain Autonomous	AILR Fully Autonomous	AILR Superhuman Autonomous
Examples	Manual, paper-based (no automation)	Word Processing, XLS, online legal docs, etc.	Query-style NLP, ML for case prediction, etc.	KBS & ML/DL for legal reasoning & analysis, etc.	Versed only in a specific legal domain	Versatile within and across all legal domains	Exceeds human-based legal reasoning
Automation	None	Legal Assist	Legal Assist	Legal Assist	Legal Advisor (law fluent)	Legal Advisor (law fluent)	Supra Legal Advisor
Status	De Facto – In Use	Widely In Use	Some In Use	Primarily Prototypes & Research-based	None As Yet	None As Yet	Indeterminate
AI-Enabled Legal Argumentation	*n/a*	*Mechanistic (Low)*	*Mechanistic (High)*	*Expressive*	*Domain Fluency*	*Full Fluency*	*Meta-Fluency*

Figure 7: AI Legal Argumentation (AILA) - Autonomous Levels of AILR by Columns *Source Author: Dr. Lance B. Eliot* V1.3

Figure 10

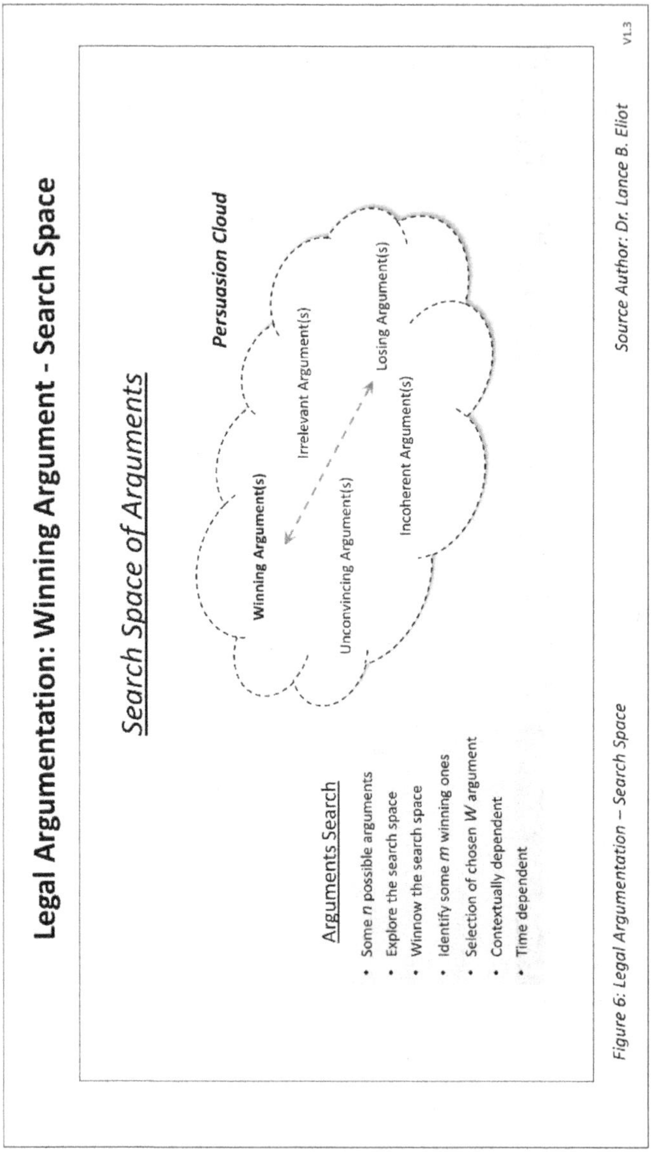
Legal Argumentation: Winning Argument - Search Space
Search Space of Arguments
Persuasion Cloud
Winning Argument(s)
Irrelevant Argument(s)
Losing Argument(s)
Unconvincing Argument(s)
Incoherent Argument(s)
Arguments Search
Some n possible arguments
Explore the search space
Winnow the search space
Identify some m winning ones
Selection of chosen W argument
Contextually dependent
Time dependent
Figure 6: Legal Argumentation – Search Space
Source Author: Dr. Lance B. Eliot
V1.3

Figure 11

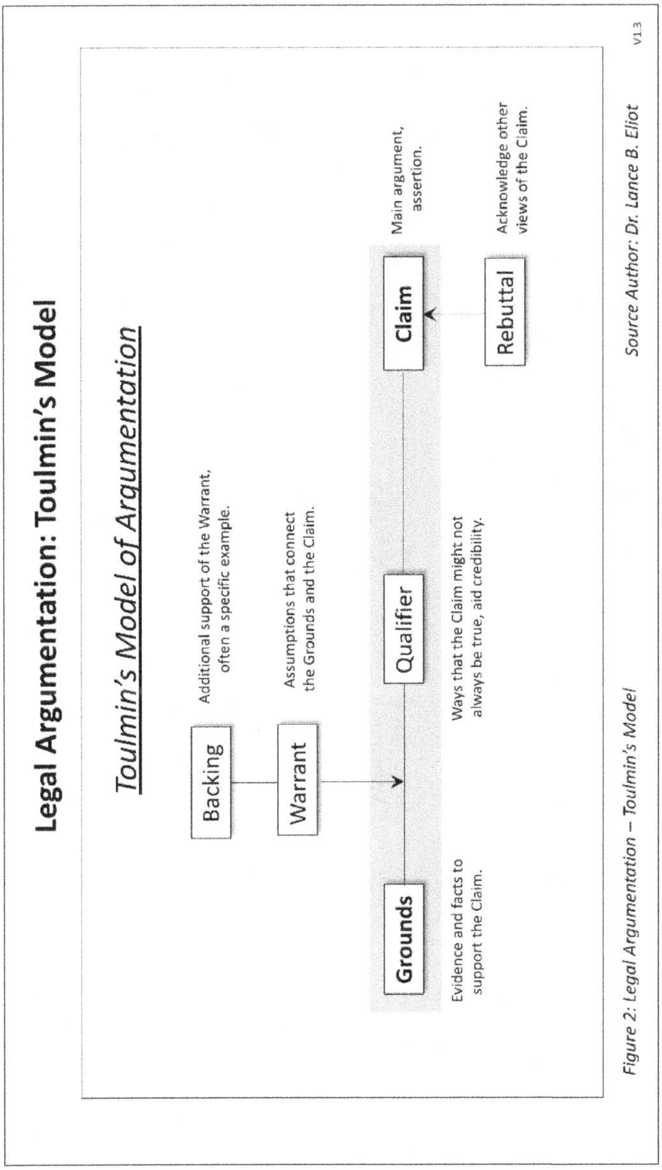
Legal Argumentation: Toulmin's Model
Toulmin's Model of Argumentation
Backing
Additional support of the Warrant, often a specific example.
Warrant
Assumptions that connect the Grounds and the Claim.
Grounds
Qualifier
Claim
Evidence and facts to support the Claim.
Ways that the Claim might not always be true, aid credibility.
Main argument, assertion.
Rebuttal
Acknowledge other views of the Claim.
Figure 2: Legal Argumentation – Toulmin's Model
Source Author: Dr. Lance B. Eliot
V1.3

Figure 12

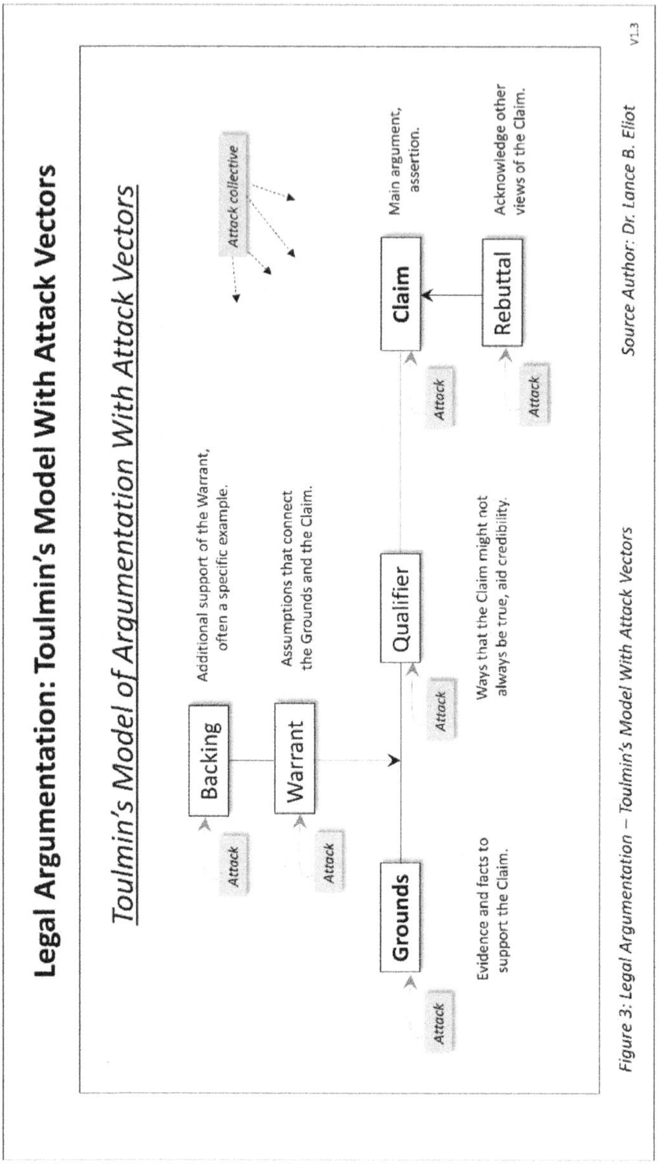
Legal Argumentation: Toulmin's Model With Attack Vectors
Toulmin's Model of Argumentation With Attack Vectors
Backing
Additional support of the Warrant, often a specific example.
Warrant
Assumptions that connect the Grounds and the Claim.
Attack collective
Grounds
Evidence and facts to support the Claim.
Qualifier
Ways that the Claim might not always be true, aid credibility.
Claim
Main argument, assertion.
Rebuttal
Acknowledge other views of the Claim.
Attack
Attack
Attack
Attack
Attack
Attack
Figure 3: Legal Argumentation – Toulmin's Model With Attack Vectors
Source Author: Dr. Lance B. Eliot
V1.3

Figure 13

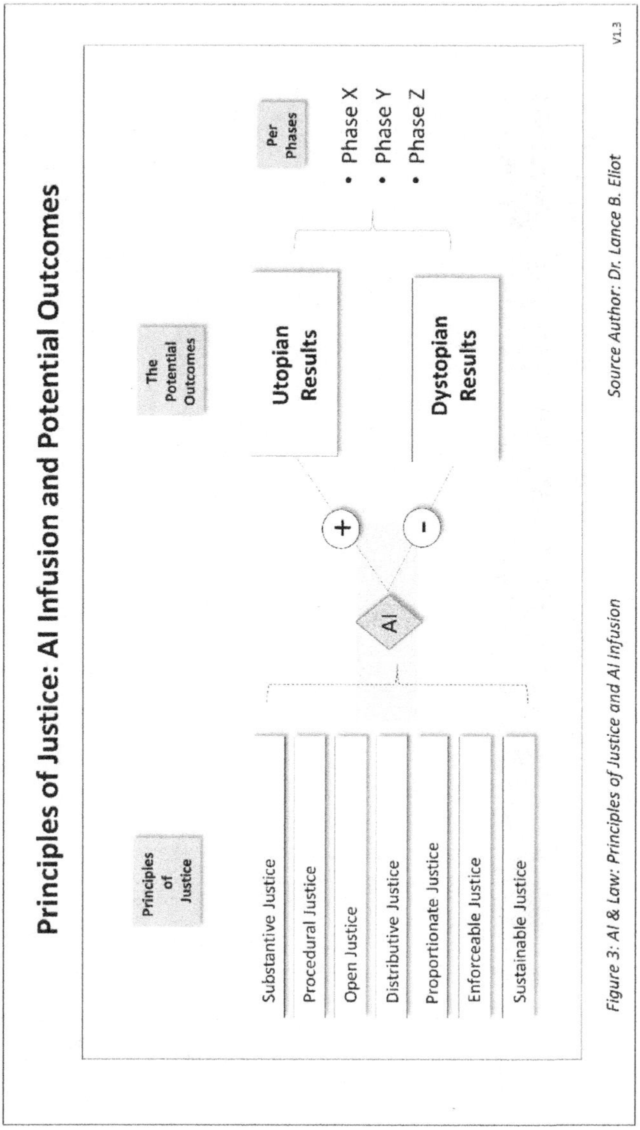
Principles of Justice: AI Infusion and Potential Outcomes
Principles of Justice
The Potential Outcomes
Per Phases
Substantive Justice
Procedural Justice
Open Justice
Distributive Justice
Proportionate Justice
Enforceable Justice
Sustainable Justice
AI
+
-
Utopian Results
Dystopian Results
• Phase X
• Phase Y
• Phase Z
Figure 3: AI & Law: Principles of Justice and AI Infusion
Source Author: Dr. Lance B. Eliot
V1.3

Figure 14

Principles of Justice and Autonomous Levels of AI Legal Reasoning (AILR)

	Level 0	Level 1	Level 2	Level 3	Level 4	Level 5	Level 6
Descriptor	No Automation	Simple Assistance Automation	Advanced Assistance Automation	Semi-Autonomous Automation	AILR Domain Autonomous	AILR Fully Autonomous	AILR Superhuman Autonomous
Substantive Justice	*Traditional*	*Traditional*	*Traditional*	Emerging	Phase X Impacts	Phase Y Impacts	Phase Z Impacts
Procedural Justice	*Traditional*	*Traditional*	*Traditional*	Emerging	Phase X Impacts	Phase Y Impacts	Phase Z Impacts
Open Justice	*Traditional*	*Traditional*	*Traditional*	Emerging	Phase X Impacts	Phase Y Impacts	Phase Z Impacts
Distributive Justice	*Traditional*	*Traditional*	*Traditional*	Emerging	Phase X Impacts	Phase Y Impacts	Phase Z Impacts
Proportionate Justice	*Traditional*	*Traditional*	*Traditional*	Emerging	Phase X Impacts	Phase Y Impacts	Phase Z Impacts
Enforceable Justice	*Traditional*	*Traditional*	*Traditional*	Emerging	Phase X Impacts	Phase Y Impacts	Phase Z Impacts
Sustainable Justice	*Traditional*	*Traditional*	*Traditional*	Emerging	Phase X Impacts	Phase Y Impacts	Phase Z Impacts

Figure 1: AI & Law – Principles of Justice and LoA AILR by Columns

Source Author: Dr. Lance B. Eliot

V1.3

Figure 15

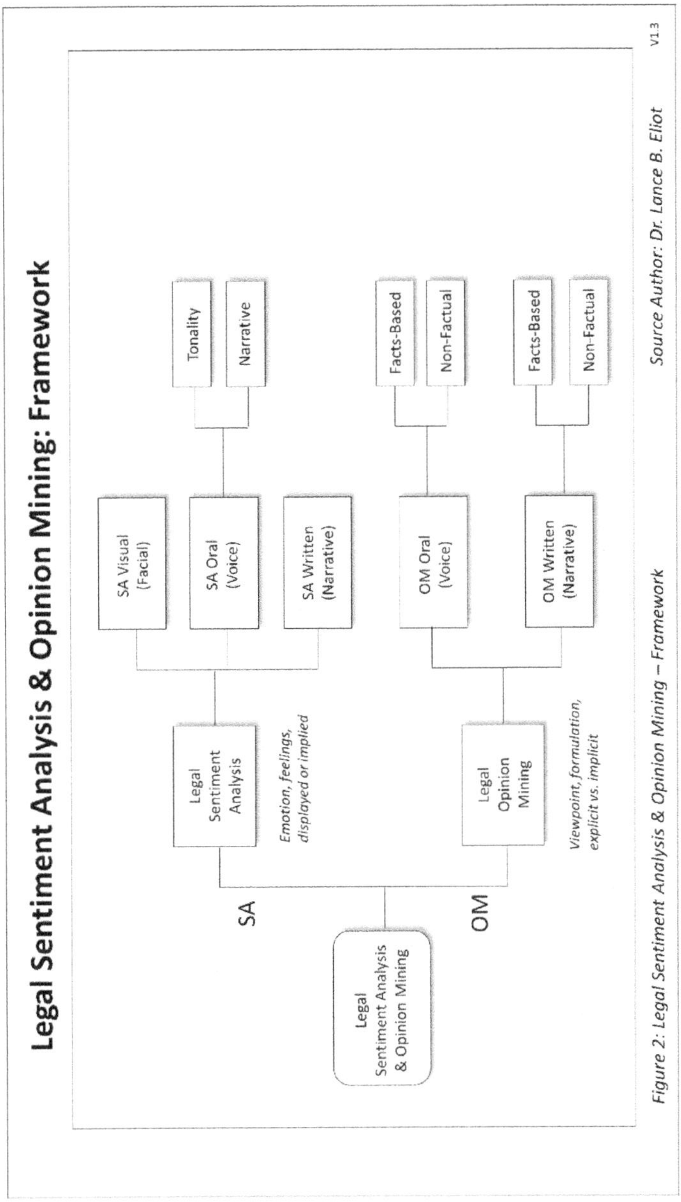
Legal Sentiment Analysis & Opinion Mining: Framework
Legal Sentiment Analysis & Opinion Mining
SA
OM
Legal Sentiment Analysis
Emotion, feelings, displayed or implied
Legal Opinion Mining
Viewpoint, formulation, explicit vs. implicit
SA Visual (Facial)
SA Oral (Voice)
SA Written (Narrative)
OM Oral (Voice)
OM Written (Narrative)
Tonality
Narrative
Facts-Based
Non-Factual
Facts-Based
Non-Factual
Figure 2: Legal Sentiment Analysis & Opinion Mining – Framework
Source Author: Dr. Lance B. Eliot
V1.3

Figure 16

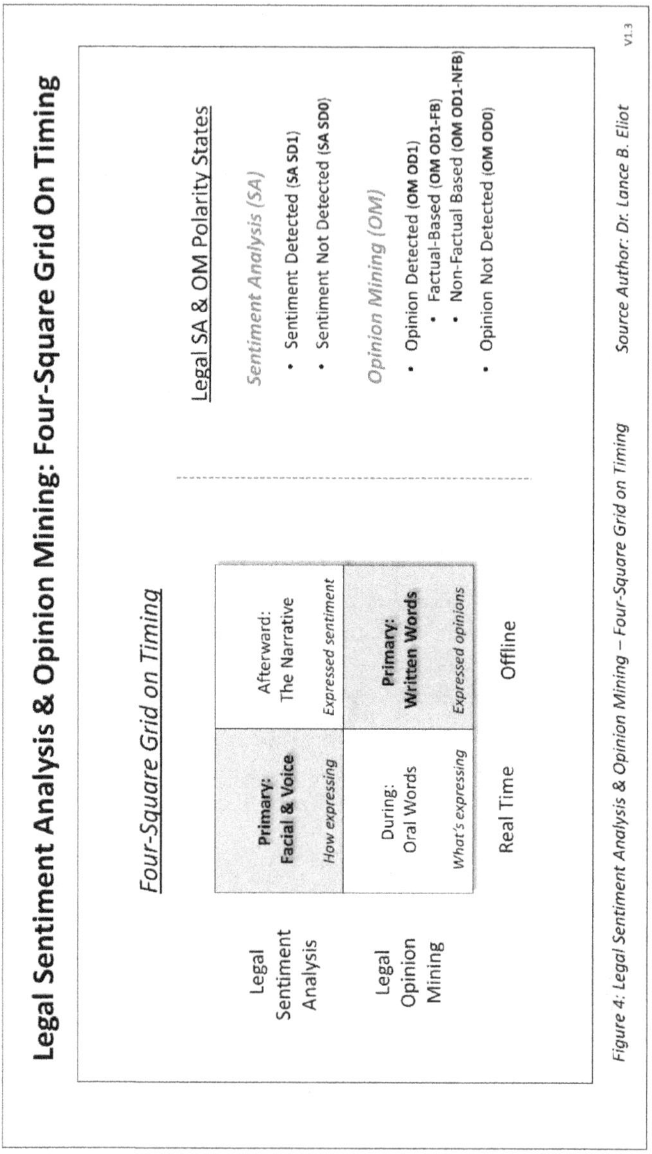
Legal Sentiment Analysis & Opinion Mining: Four-Square Grid On Timing
Four-Square Grid on Timing
Legal Sentiment Analysis
Legal Opinion Mining
Primary: Facial & Voice
How expressing
Afterward: The Narrative
Expressed sentiment
During: Oral Words
What's expressing
Primary: Written Words
Expressed opinions
Real Time
Offline
Legal SA & OM Polarity States
Sentiment Analysis (SA)
Sentiment Detected (SA SD1)
Sentiment Not Detected (SA SD0)
Opinion Mining (OM)
Opinion Detected (OM OD1)
Factual-Based (OM OD1-FB)
Non-Factual Based (OM OD1-NFB)
Opinion Not Detected (OM OD0)
Figure 4: Legal Sentiment Analysis & Opinion Mining – Four-Square Grid on Timing
Source Author: Dr. Lance B. Eliot
V1.3

Figure 17

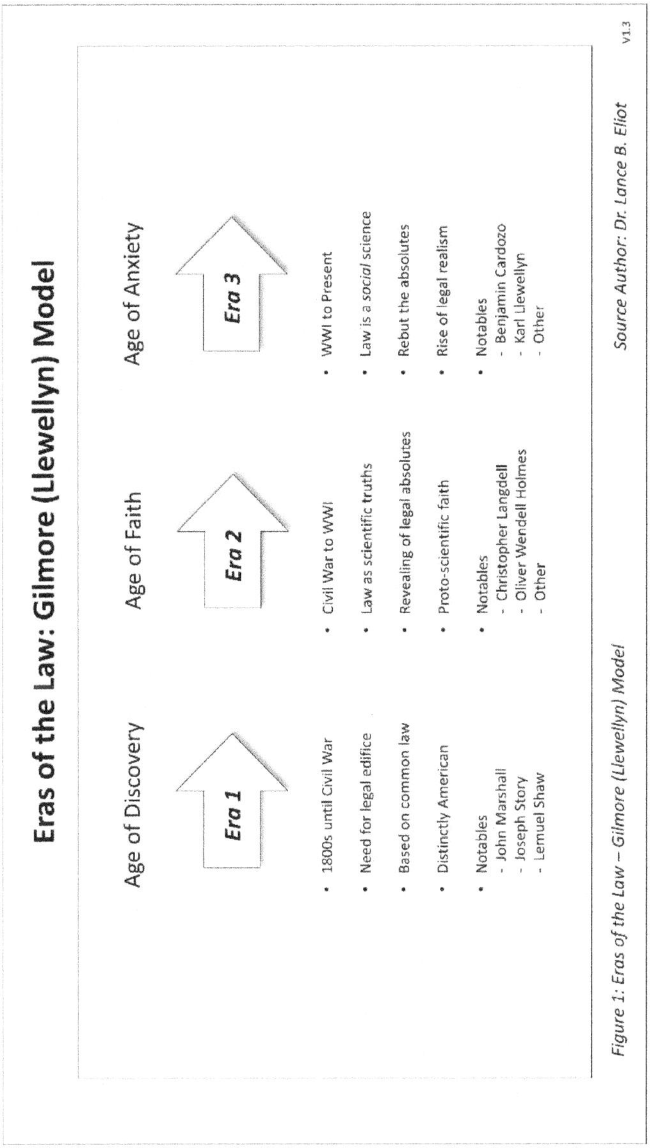
Eras of the Law: Gilmore (Llewellyn) Model
Age of Discovery
Era 1
1800s until Civil War
Need for legal edifice
Based on common law
Distinctly American
Notables
- John Marshall
- Joseph Story
- Lemuel Shaw
Age of Faith
Era 2
Civil War to WWI
Law as scientific truths
Revealing of legal absolutes
Proto-scientific faith
Notables
- Christopher Langdell
- Oliver Wendell Holmes
- Other
Age of Anxiety
Era 3
WWI to Present
Law is a social science
Rebut the absolutes
Rise of legal realism
Notables
- Benjamin Cardozo
- Karl Llewellyn
- Other
Figure 1: Eras of the Law – Gilmore (Llewellyn) Model
Source Author: Dr. Lance B. Eliot
V1.3

Figure 18

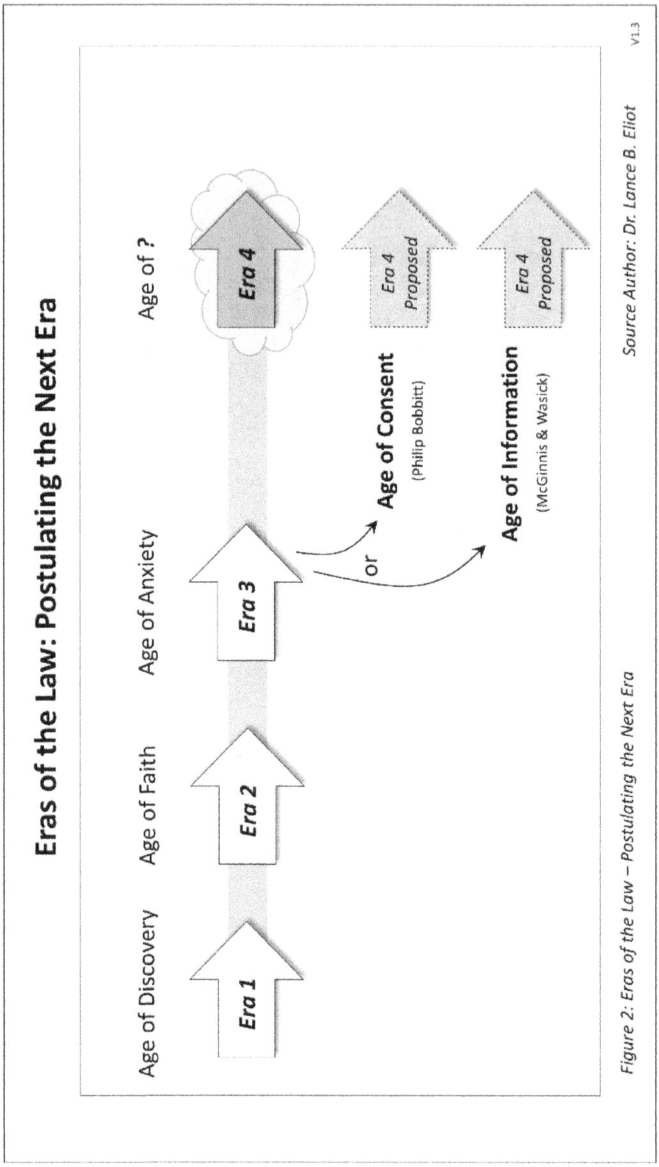
Eras of the Law: Postulating the Next Era
Age of Discovery
Age of Faith
Age of Anxiety
Age of ?
Era 1
Era 2
Era 3
Era 4
or
Age of Consent
(Philip Bobbitt)
Era 4 Proposed
Age of Information
(McGinnis & Wasick)
Era 4 Proposed
Figure 2: Eras of the Law – Postulating the Next Era
Source Author: Dr. Lance B. Eliot
V1.3

Figure 19

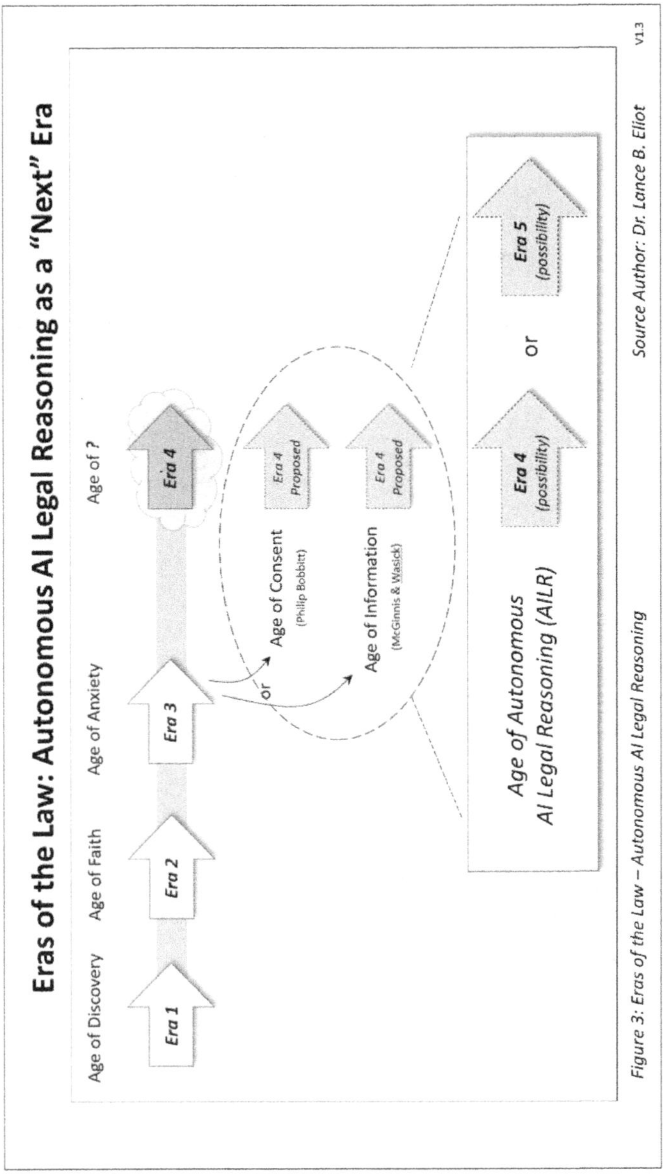
Eras of the Law: Autonomous AI Legal Reasoning as a "Next" Era
Age of Discovery
Age of Faith
Age of Anxiety
Age of ?
Era 1
Era 2
Era 3
Era 4
or
Age of Consent
(Philip Bobbitt)
Era 4 Proposed
Age of Information
(McGinnis & Wasick)
Era 4 Proposed
Age of Autonomous AI Legal Reasoning (AILR)
Era 4 (possibility)
or
Era 5 (possibility)
Figure 3: Eras of the Law – Autonomous AI Legal Reasoning
Source Author: Dr. Lance B. Eliot
V1.3

Figure 20

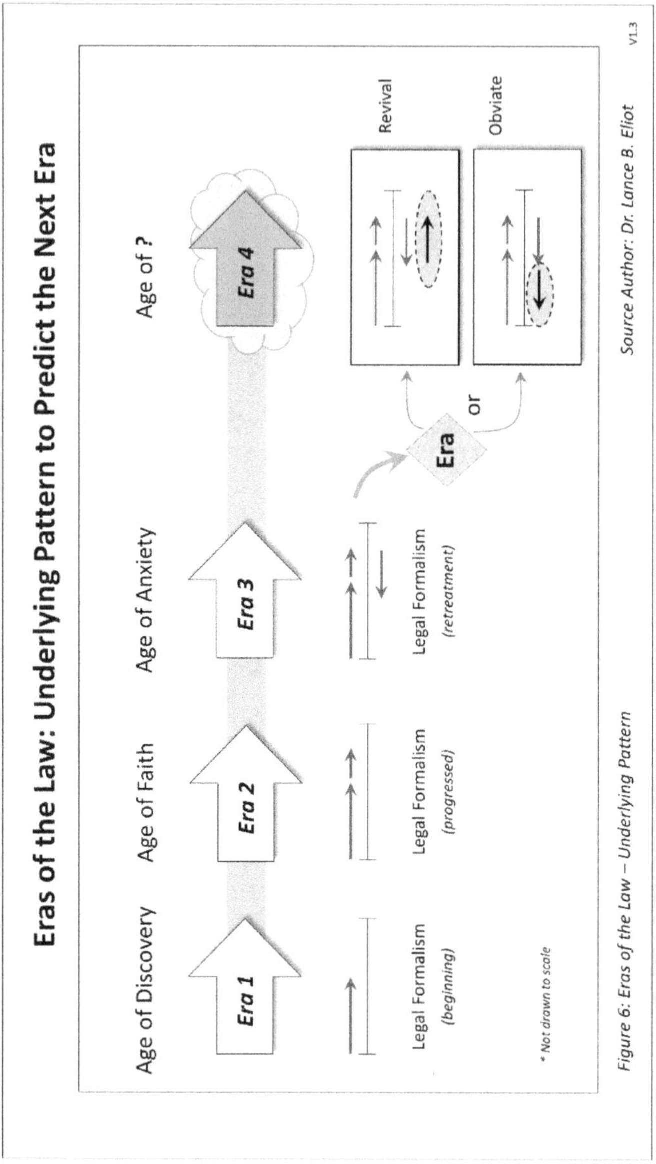
Eras of the Law: Underlying Pattern to Predict the Next Era
Age of Discovery
Age of Faith
Age of Anxiety
Age of ?
Era 1
Era 2
Era 3
Era 4
Legal Formalism
(beginning)
Legal Formalism
(progressed)
Legal Formalism
(retreatment)
Era
or
Revival
Obviate
* Not drawn to scale
Figure 6: Eras of the Law – Underlying Pattern
Source Author: Dr. Lance B. Eliot
V1.3

Figure 21

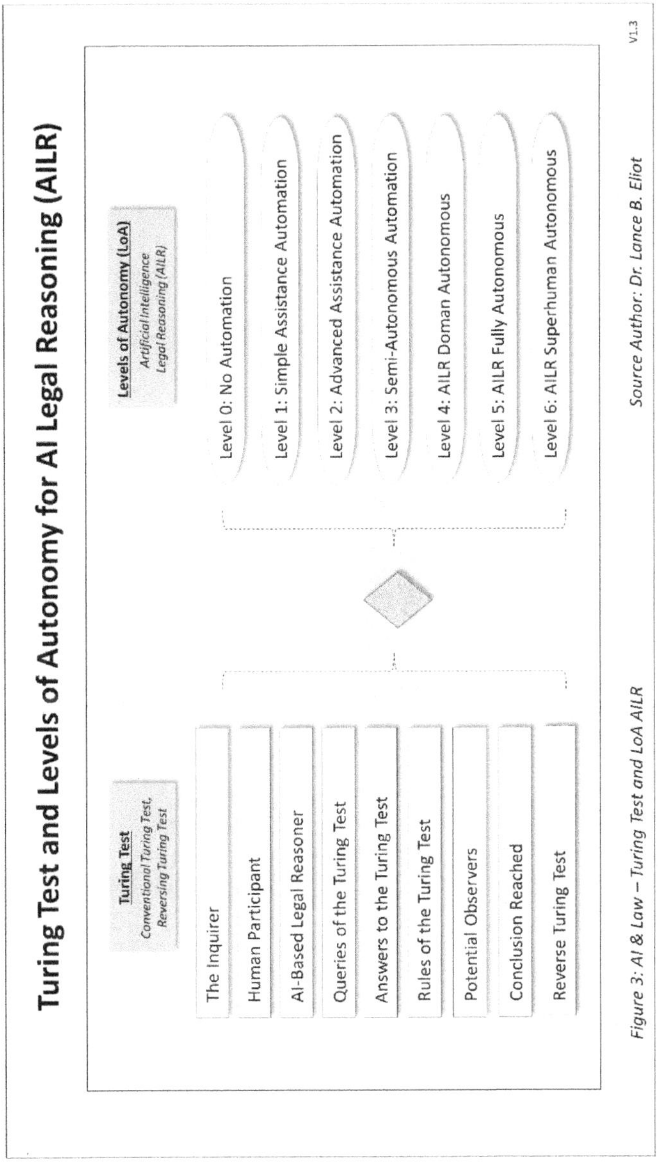

Figure 3: AI & Law – Turing Test and LoA AILR

Figure 22

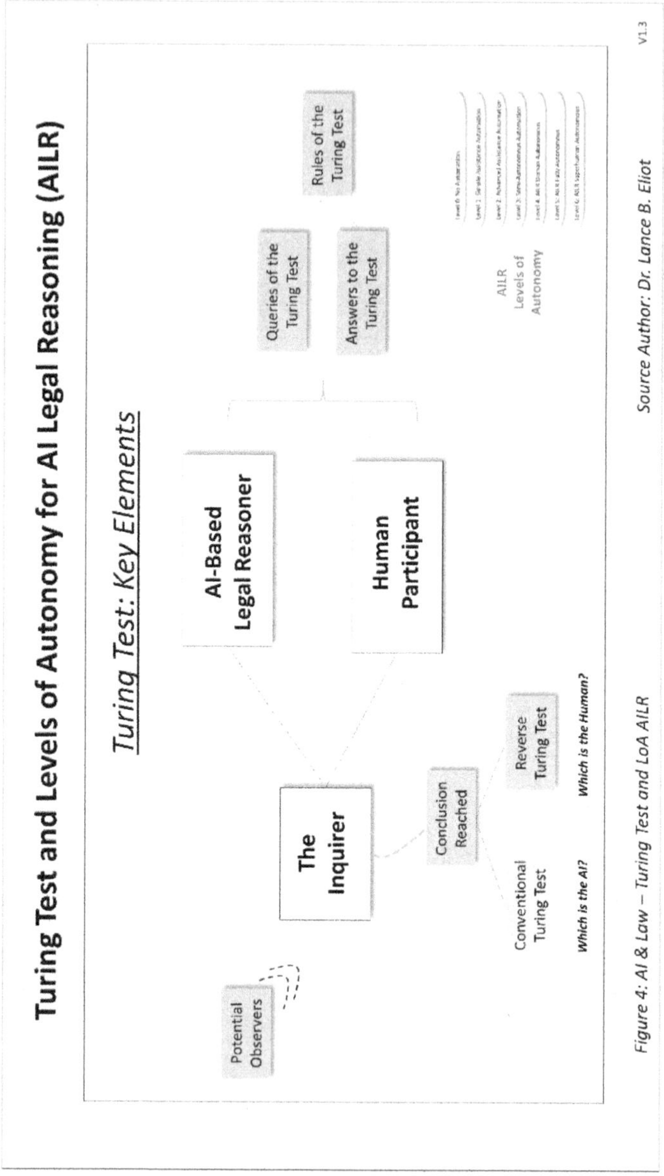
Turing Test and Levels of Autonomy for AI Legal Reasoning (AILR)
Turing Test: Key Elements
Potential Observers
The Inquirer
AI-Based Legal Reasoner
Human Participant
Queries of the Turing Test
Answers to the Turing Test
Rules of the Turing Test
Conclusion Reached
Conventional Turing Test
Reverse Turing Test
Which is the AI?
Which is the Human?
AILR Levels of Autonomy
Figure 4: AI & Law – Turing Test and LoA AILR
Source Author: Dr. Lance B. Eliot
V1.3

Figure 23

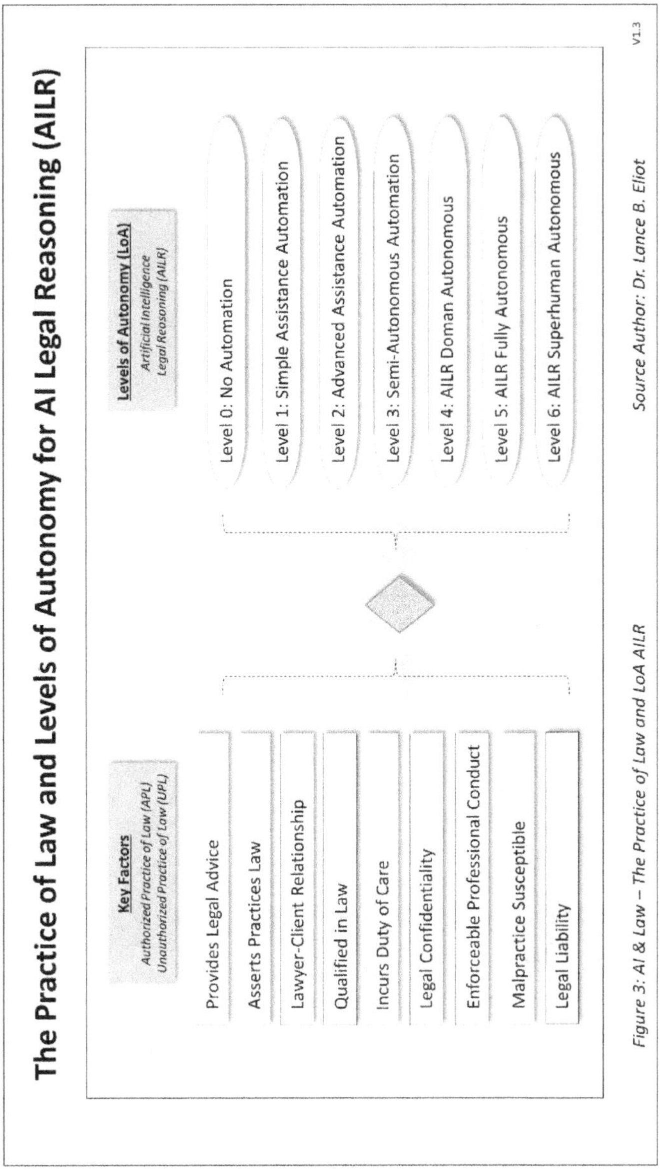

Figure 3: AI & Law – The Practice of Law and LoA AILR

Source Author: Dr. Lance B. Eliot

Figure 24

Strawman Variant

The Practice of Law and Autonomous Levels of AI Legal Reasoning (AILR)

	Level 0	Level 1	Level 2	Level 3	Level 4	Level 5	Level 6
Descriptor	No Automation	Simple Assistance Automation	Advanced Assistance Automation	Semi-Autonomous Automation	AILR Domain Autonomous	AILR Fully Autonomous	AILR Superhuman Autonomous
Provides Legal Advice	n/a	No	Maybe	Yes	Yes	Yes	Yes Plus
Asserts Practices Law	n/a	No	No	No	Yes	Yes	Yes Plus
Lawyer-Client Relationship	n/a	No	No	No	Partial	Yes	Yes
Qualified in Law	n/a	No	No	Minimal	Partial	Yes	Yes Plus
Incurs Duty of Care	n/a	No	No	No	Likely	Yes	Yes
Legal Confidentiality	n/a	No	No	No	Likely	Yes	Yes
Enforceable Prof Conduct	n/a	No	No	No	Likely	Yes	Yes
Malpractice Susceptible	n/a	No	No	No	Likely	Yes	Yes
Legal Liability	n/a	No	Maybe	Likely	Likely	Yes	Yes

Figure 1: AI & Law – The Practice of Law and LoA AILR by Columns *Source Author: Dr. Lance B. Eliot* V1.3

Figure 25

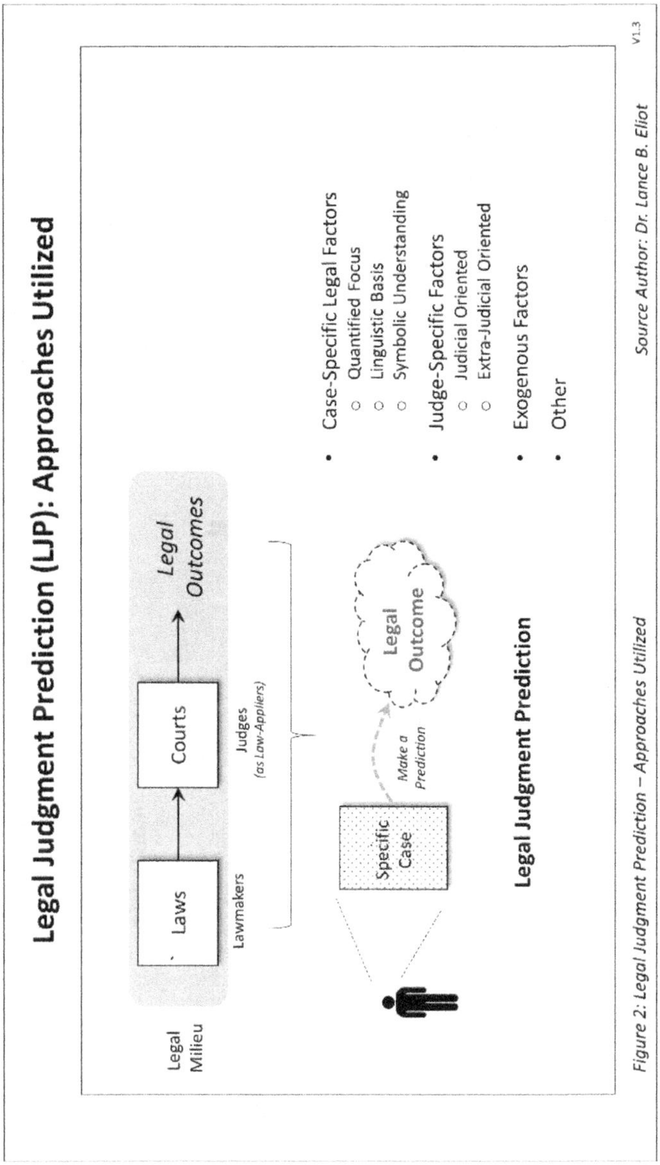
Legal Judgment Prediction (LJP): Approaches Utilized
Legal Milieu
Laws
Courts
Legal Outcomes
Lawmakers
Judges (as Law-Appliers)
Specific Case
Make a Prediction
Legal Outcome
Legal Judgment Prediction
Case-Specific Legal Factors
Quantified Focus
Linguistic Basis
Symbolic Understanding
Judge-Specific Factors
Judicial Oriented
Extra-Judicial Oriented
Exogenous Factors
Other
Figure 2: Legal Judgment Prediction – Approaches Utilized
Source Author: Dr. Lance B. Eliot
V1.3

Figure 26

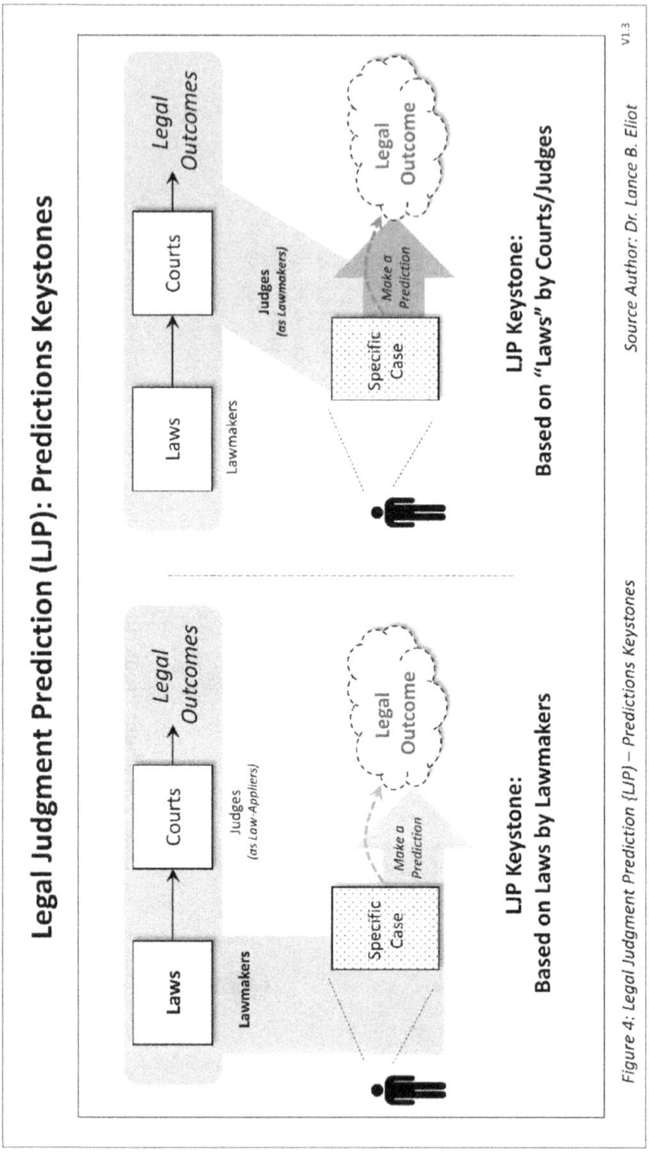
Legal Judgment Prediction (LJP): Predictions Keystones
Laws
Courts
Legal Outcomes
Lawmakers
Judges (as Law-Appliers)
Specific Case
Make a Prediction
Legal Outcome
LJP Keystone: Based on Laws by Lawmakers
Laws
Courts
Legal Outcomes
Lawmakers
Judges (as Lawmakers)
Specific Case
Make a Prediction
Legal Outcome
LJP Keystone: Based on "Laws" by Courts/Judges
Figure 4: Legal Judgment Prediction (LJP) – Predictions Keystones
Source Author: Dr. Lance B. Eliot
V1.3

Figure 27

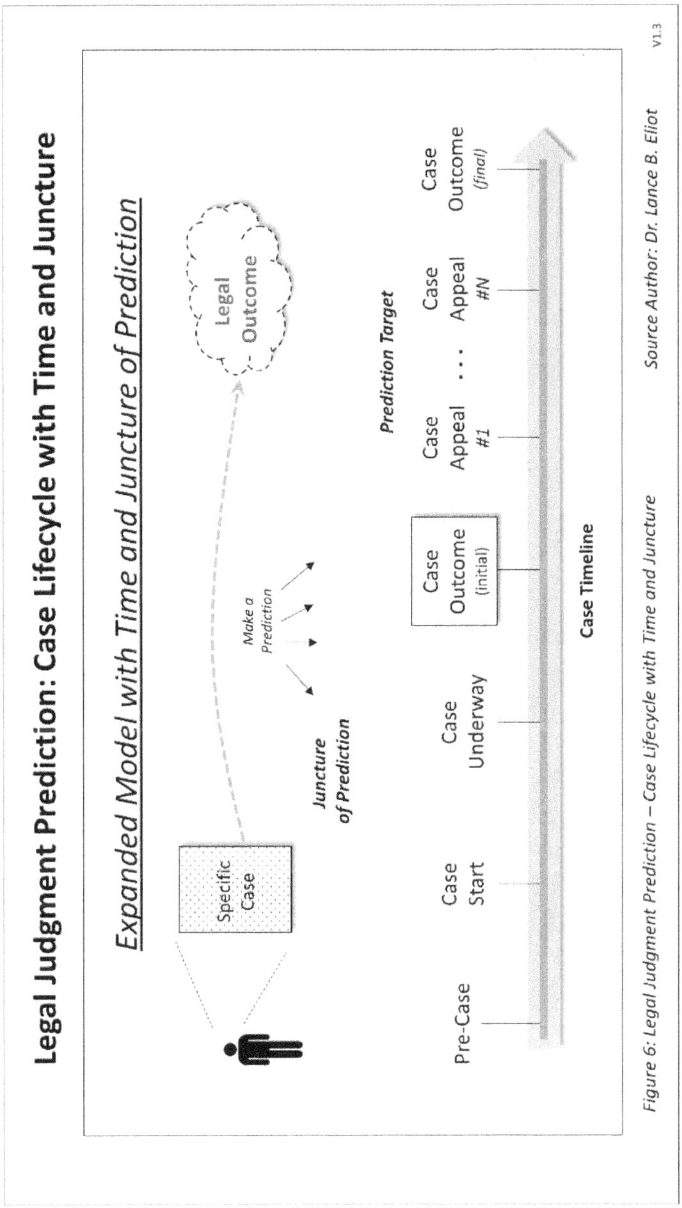
Legal Judgment Prediction: Case Lifecycle with Time and Juncture
Expanded Model with Time and Juncture of Prediction
Specific Case
Legal Outcome
Make a Prediction
Juncture of Prediction
Prediction Target
Pre-Case
Case Start
Case Underway
Case Outcome (initial)
Case Appeal #1
. . .
Case Appeal #N
Case Outcome (final)
Case Timeline
Figure 6: Legal Judgment Prediction – Case Lifecycle with Time and Juncture
Source Author: Dr. Lance B. Eliot
V1.3

Figure 28

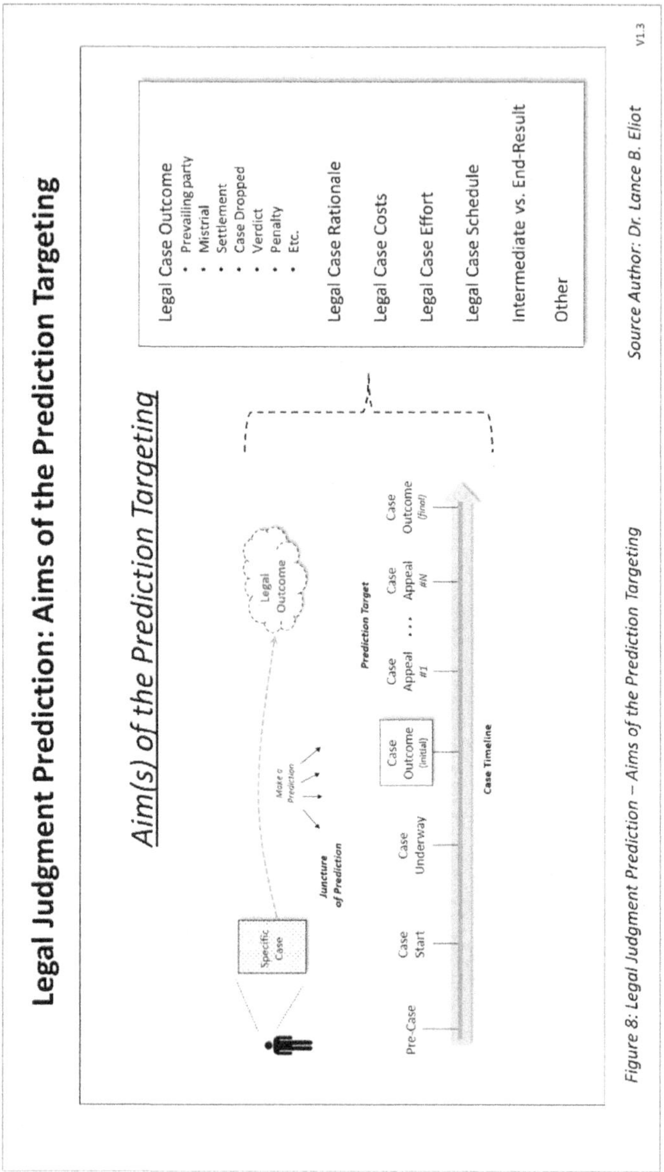
Legal Judgment Prediction: Aims of the Prediction Targeting
Aim(s) of the Prediction Targeting
Specific Case
Juncture of Prediction
Make a Prediction
Legal Outcome
Prediction Target
Pre-Case
Case Start
Case Underway
Case Outcome (initial)
Case Appeal #1
. . .
Case Appeal #N
Case Outcome (final)
Case Timeline
Legal Case Outcome
• Prevailing party
• Mistrial
• Settlement
• Case Dropped
• Verdict
• Penalty
• Etc.
Legal Case Rationale
Legal Case Costs
Legal Case Effort
Legal Case Schedule
Intermediate vs. End-Result
Other
Figure 8: Legal Judgment Prediction – Aims of the Prediction Targeting
Source Author: Dr. Lance B. Eliot
V1.3

Figure 29

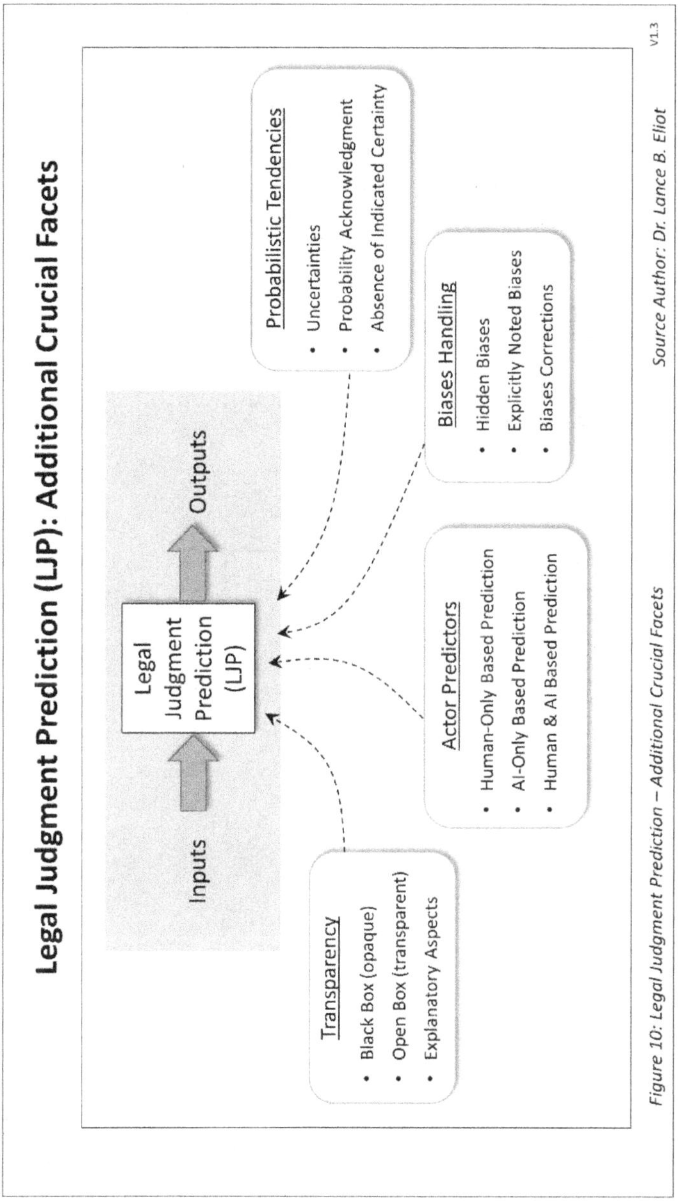
Legal Judgment Prediction (LJP): Additional Crucial Facets
Inputs
Legal Judgment Prediction (LJP)
Outputs
Transparency
• Black Box (opaque)
• Open Box (transparent)
• Explanatory Aspects
Actor Predictors
• Human-Only Based Prediction
• AI-Only Based Prediction
• Human & AI Based Prediction
Biases Handling
• Hidden Biases
• Explicitly Noted Biases
• Biases Corrections
Probabilistic Tendencies
• Uncertainties
• Probability Acknowledgment
• Absence of Indicated Certainty
Figure 10: Legal Judgment Prediction – Additional Crucial Facets
Source Author: Dr. Lance B. Eliot
V1.3

Figure 30

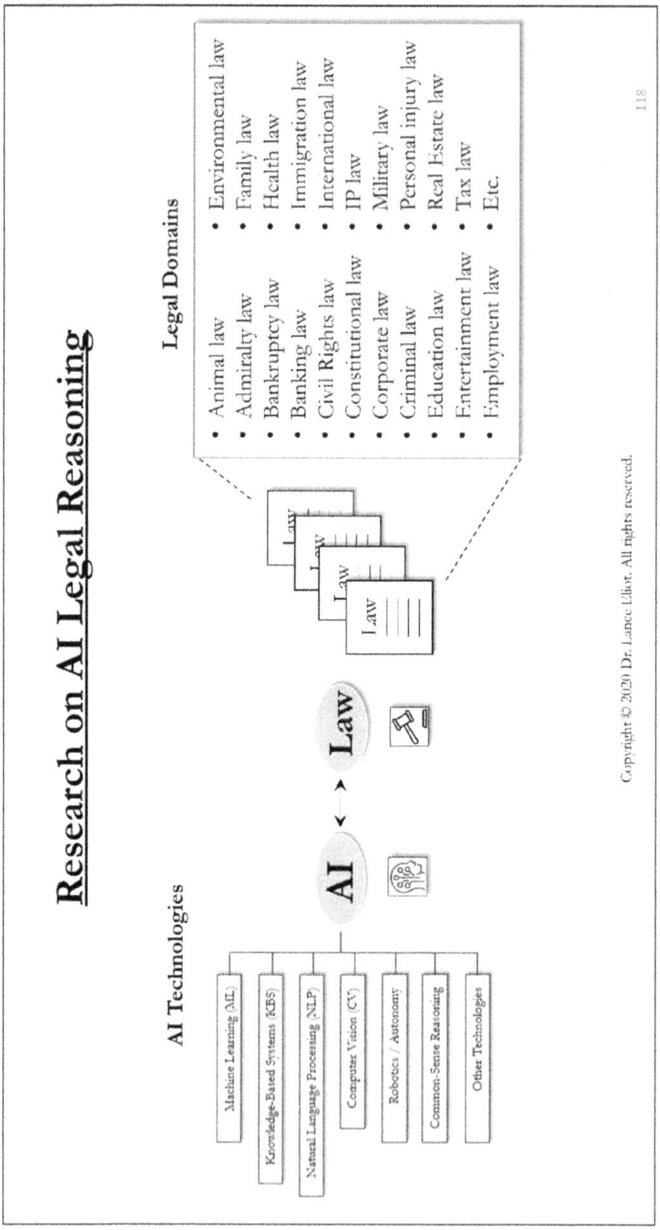
Research on AI Legal Reasoning
AI Technologies
Machine Learning (ML)
Knowledge-Based Systems (KBS)
Natural Language Processing (NLP)
Computer Vision (CV)
Robotics / Autonomy
Common-Sense Reasoning
Other Technologies
AI
Law
Law
Law
Law
Law
Legal Domains
• Animal law
• Admiralty law
• Bankruptcy law
• Banking law
• Civil Rights law
• Constitutional law
• Corporate law
• Criminal law
• Education law
• Entertainment law
• Employment law
• Environmental law
• Family law
• Health law
• Immigration law
• International law
• IP law
• Military law
• Personal injury law
• Real Estate law
• Tax law
• Etc.
Copyright © 2020 Dr. Lance Eliot. All rights reserved.
118

Figure 31

ABOUT THE AUTHOR

Dr. Lance B. Eliot, Ph.D., MBA is a globally recognized AI expert and thought leader, an invited Stanford Fellow at Stanford University, an experienced top executive and corporate leader, a successful entrepreneur, and a noted scholar on AI, including that his Forbes and AI Trends columns have amassed over 4 million views, his books on AI are ranked in the Top 10 of all-time AI books, his journal articles are widely cited, and he has developed and implemented numerous AI systems.

He currently serves as the Chief AI Scientist at Techbruim, Inc. and has over twenty years of industry experience including serving as a corporate officer in billion-dollar sized firms and was a partner in a major consulting firm. He is also a successful entrepreneur having founded, ran, and sold several high-tech related businesses.

Dr. Eliot previously hosted the popular radio show *Technotrends* that was also available on American Airlines flights via their in-flight audio program, he has made appearances on CNN, has been a frequent speaker at industry conferences, and his podcasts have been downloaded over 150,000 times.

A former professor at the University of Southern California (USC), he founded and led an innovative research lab on Artificial Intelligence. He also previously served on the faculty of the University of California Los Angeles (UCLA) and was a visiting professor at other major universities. He was elected to the International Board of the Society for Information Management (SIM), a prestigious association of over 3,000 high-tech executives worldwide.

He has performed extensive community service, including serving as Senior Science Adviser to the Congressional Vice-Chair of the Congressional Committee on Science & Technology. He has served on the Board of the OC Science & Engineering Fair (OCSEF), where he is also has been a Grand Sweepstakes judge, and likewise served as a judge for the Intel International SEF (ISEF). He served as the Vice-Chair of the Association for Computing Machinery (ACM) Chapter, a prestigious association of computer scientists. Dr. Eliot has been a shark tank judge for the USC Mark Stevens Center for Innovation on start-up pitch competitions and served as a mentor for several incubators and accelerators in Silicon Valley and in Silicon Beach.

Dr. Eliot holds a Ph.D. from USC, MBA, and Bachelor's in Computer Science, and earned the CDP, CCP, CSP, CDE, and CISA certification.

Companion Book By Dr. Lance Eliot

"Artificial Intelligence and Legal Reasoning Essentials"

ISBN 978-1-73460165-7

Chapters

Available on Amazon and via other online book sellers

Companion Book By Dr. Lance Eliot

"Artificial Intelligence and LegalTech Essentials"

ISBN 978-1-7346016-3-3

Chapters

Available on Amazon and via other online book sellers

Companion Book By Dr. Lance Eliot

"Decisive Essays On AI And Law"

ISBN 978-1-73630310-8

Chapters

Available on Amazon and via other online book sellers

Companion Book By Dr. Lance Eliot

"Incisive Research On AI And Law"

ISBN 978-1-73630311-5

Chapters

Available on Amazon and via other online book sellers

Companion Book By Dr. Lance Eliot

"Ingenious Essays On AI And Law"

ISBN 978-1-73630312-2

Chapters

Available on Amazon and via other online book seller

Companion Book By Dr. Lance Eliot

"Compelling Essays On AI And Law"

ISBN 978-1-73630313-9

Chapters

Available on Amazon and via other online book sellers

Companion Book By Dr. Lance Eliot

"Topnotch Essays On AI And Law"

ISBN 978-1-73630314-6

Chapters

Available on Amazon and via other online book sellers

Companion Book By Dr. Lance Eliot

"Trendsetting Essays On AI And Law"

ISBN 978-1-95-738601-0

Chapters

Available on Amazon and via other online book sellers

Companion Book By Dr. Lance Eliot

"Pioneering Essays On AI And Law"

ISBN 978-1-95-738602-7

Chapters

Available on Amazon and via other online book sellers

Companion Book By Dr. Lance Eliot

"Trailblazing Essays On AI And Law"

ISBN 978-1-95-738602-7

Chapters

Available on Amazon and via other online book sellers

Companion Book By Dr. Lance Eliot

"Leading Edge Essays On AI And Law"

ISBN 978-1-95-738604-1

Chapters

Available on Amazon and via other online book sellers

ADDENDUM

Thanks for reading this book and I hope you will continue your interest in the field of AI & Law

---

For my free podcasts about AI & Law:

https://ai-law.libsyn.com/website

Those podcasts are also available on Spotify, iTunes, etc.

For the latest on AI & Law see my website:

www.ai-law.legal

To follow me on Twitter:

https://twitter.com/LanceEliot

For my in-depth book on AI & Law:

AI And Legal Reasoning Essentials

www.amazon.com/gp/product/1734601655/

Made in the USA
Monee, IL
05 November 2026

67808610R00125